CHANGING BAD

HARNESSING THE POWER OF MOTIVATION

EZEKIEL DANIEL

Changing Bad: Harnessing the Power of Motivation

Published by Ezekiel Daniel

Augusta, Georgia

ISBN: 979-8-9899217-5-1(Hardcover Edition)

ISBN: 979-8-9899217-6-8 (Paperback Edition)

ISBN: 979-8-9899217-7-5 (Audiobook Edition)

Printed in the United States of America

First Edition, 2025

DEDICATION PAGE

Dedicated to those who dare to dream, have the courage to act, and never stop believing in themselves.

CONTENTS

PREFACE

CONTRACT

You are entering a binding contract—a solemn yet empowering commitment to embark on a transformative journey of positive healing and dynamic change. This journey is your pledge to yourself, a deliberate decision to revitalize your mind, strengthen your body, and nourish your soul. You are now bound to an understanding that life offers no second chances, no resets, and no revisions. This moment marks your conscious decision, your signed agreement to step boldly into action, driving profound transformation within and around you.

As you progress through these pages, you commit to engaging deeply with essential principles designed to ignite immediate action, uncover your intrinsic value, and fortify the resilience necessary to surmount life's inevitable challenges. Your contract requires you to actively engage your mind, developing strategic thinking that empowers you to manifest your full potential. You willingly pledge to embrace adaptability, navigating life's uncertainties with grace and agility, confidently turning obstacles into opportunities.

Through this binding commitment, courage will become your constant companion, empowering you to confront change and uncertainty with an open heart and fearless determination. You promise to allow love to guide you, fostering authentic connections, nurturing meaningful relationships, and contributing positively to the lives of others, enriching your soul and elevating your purpose.

Your contract mandates cultivating a foundation of logic and disciplined thinking, providing clarity and consistency in the face of life's complexities. Discipline is now your ally, reinforcing your commitments and fueling sustained personal and professional growth. You willingly embrace change as a catalyst for evolution, infusing bravery into every decision and action, refusing to shrink in the face of challenges.

By committing to this journey, you bind yourself to honor nature's balance and restorative wisdom, grounding yourself in harmony and peace. Your newfound awareness of humanity compels compassionate interactions, uplifting yourself and everyone around you. Recognizing the necessity of calculated risks, you commit to boldly stepping toward extraordinary outcomes, balancing ambition with attentive self-care and holistic well-being.

Your agreement involves living with perpetual optimism and nurturing hope, crafting a vision that sees possibilities in every challenge and opportunities in every uncertainty. You promise to transform your perspective through mindful vigilance, safeguarding your mental and emotional clarity. Your actions will be deliberate, your decisions purposeful, and your goals passionately pursued, anchored by unwavering commitment.

Self-care is integral to this contract, acknowledging that nurturing your wellness is essential for lasting success. Sacrifice is not viewed as a loss, but as a strategic investment toward greater achievements. You will embrace boldness, harnessing ingenuity to creatively overcome obstacles, maximize opportunities, and reshape the narrative of your life.

This binding agreement empowers you to draw upon inner strength, guiding you through life's turbulence with tranquility and steadfast integrity. Every step you take will be underscored by honesty, credibility, and trust, forging a life rich with passion, purpose, and positivity.

Your signature on this contract signifies your readiness to commit fully to personal excellence, lifelong learning, and transformative growth. You are bound to rise above mediocrity, actively shaping your destiny with unwavering dedication, strategic action, and profound self-awareness.

Let Us Begin!

Signature By...

Witness Signature..

INVESTMENT

Give me six months of work for a lifetime of value.

S uccess is not built overnight—it is cultivated over time through dedication and strategic effort. Short-term sacrifice fuels long-term gain. Whether in personal development, career growth, or financial planning, consistent investment in the present leads to exponential rewards in the future. Think of every effort as a seed planted; with patience and care, it will yield abundant fruit. Stay committed—results may not be immediate, but they will be well worth it in the end.

There is a quiet power in the discipline of consistency—of giving your all to something not for the immediate reward, but for the life that unfolds afterward. Imagine offering six months of focused, intentional work to your goal. What might that yield? What if, by committing wholeheartedly to growth, sacrifice, and improvement now, you could alter the rest of your journey in profound ways? This idea isn't about magic or shortcuts. It's about embracing the grind.

It's about the late nights filled with effort when no one is watching, the early mornings of reflection, and the moments of discomfort that make you question your commitment. These are not setbacks—they are confirmations that you are investing in something real.

The world teaches us to crave instant gratification. We're told that success should be fast, flashy, and always visible. But true investment is more subtle. It's found in the quiet decision to show up, every day, even when progress feels invisible. It's found in the hours of preparation, the missed parties, the held-back purchases, the sleepless planning—and the belief that the return will come, even if you can't yet see it.

Think of your efforts as compound interest. Each bit of time, energy, and discipline adds up.

One day you look up, and what seemed small—just six months—has created ripple effects far beyond the original effort. Relationships are strengthened, knowledge becomes wisdom, discipline turns into mastery. This isn't just about money or careers. It's about anything worth having—health, faith, trust, confidence. These are not handed out freely; they are earned in installments. Your investment becomes a down payment on a future self you can be proud of.

So, give six months. Give six months of work, of commitment, of belief, of discomfort, of intentional sacrifice. And in return, claim the value that lasts a lifetime—a version of yourself you built with purpose, forged through effort, and backed by your own unwavering belief that it was all worth it. Because it is. And it will be.

PROACTIVITY

If not today, when; if not when, why? There is never a better time to get the job done.

T he greatest barrier to achievement is often hesitation. Waiting for the "perfect time" is an illusion—there will always be challenges, uncertainties, and doubts. Procrastination delays progress, while action moves us forward. Taking the first step, however small, creates momentum. The sooner we begin, the sooner we reap the rewards of our efforts. A proactive mindset shifts us from passive waiting to active creation, ensuring we take charge of our own success.

The clock is always ticking, even when we pretend it's not. We often wait—wait for clarity, for motivation, for resources, for someone else to say it's time. We convince ourselves that the right moment is around the corner, that we'll know when it arrives. But more often than not, the "perfect" time never comes. The road stays foggy. The calendar remains full. And in that hesitation, time slips through our fingers. Proactivity is the counter to that drift. It's the act of choosing to move forward despite uncertainty, despite discomfort, despite fear. It's looking at your dream, your goal, your unfinished work and saying, I will not wait for permission to begin.

When you ask yourself, If not today, when?, you confront the truth: most of what you seek lies just on the other side of motion.

The first action—writing the first sentence, making the call, setting the meeting, packing the bag—breaks the inertia. It is in doing that clarity begins to arrive. Not before. The danger of inaction is that it becomes habitual. Each day you delay becomes evidence that the task can wait. Days turn into weeks, and momentum—once easily gained—is now buried under excuses. Inaction becomes its own kind of decision: a passive surrender to the idea that you have time to spare. But what if you didn't? What if today was the only day you could make progress? What if this moment was as clear as it was ever going to get?

A proactive life is not about overplanning or perfectionism. It's about willingness. It's the mindset that says, "even if I don't have everything I need, I'll begin with what I have." It's resourceful. It's gritty. It's resilient. When you act—when you initiate rather than wait—you unlock your power. You become the architect rather than the observer. You stop reacting to life and start directing it.

So ask again: If not today, when? If not when, why? The answers may be uncomfortable. But they are always revealing. Because there's never a better time to start than now. And once you do, you'll wonder why you ever waited.

TRUST

When your voice is insufficient, lean in on your faith.

There will be moments in life when words fail, reasoning falls short, and influence is insufficient. In those times, trust becomes our greatest ally. Trust in ourselves, in the process, and in the unseen forces that guide us. Faith—whether in a higher power, the universe, or our own resilience—anchors us when logic wavers. Sometimes, the best course of action is not to force an outcome but to believe that everything is aligning as it should. In that trust, we find clarity, strength, and peace.

There is a threshold where action ends and surrender begins. It is the space between effort and outcome, the moment when we've done all we can—spoken our truth, made our moves, and taken our stand—and yet, the result is still uncertain. That is the moment when trust becomes everything.

We are taught to push, strategize, calculate our way to success. And often, that works. But what happens when the door won't open no matter how hard we knock? What happens when logic and persuasion reach their limits—when even our loudest voice can't carry far enough? In those moments, lean into something deeper: faith. Not because you've given up—but because you've given everything.

Trust isn't passive. It is an act of strength to release control when control is no longer possible.

It's a declaration that, even in silence, something is still working on your behalf. This kind of trust is multi-layered: trust in yourself, trust in the process, trust in something greater. Trust doesn't silence your voice; it calms the noise of doubt around it. It helps you breathe when the outcome is out of reach. It helps you stand still when rushing forward will do more harm than good. It is the quiet power that reminds you: you've done your part. Let the rest unfold. Sometimes, the most powerful thing you can do is not to speak louder or move faster—but to trust deeper.

CAUTION

Knowing the truth does not always offer you the upper hand; tread carefully when the truth is not enough.

Truth is powerful, but it is not always the winning card in life's complex game. There are moments when knowing too much can be burdensome, and revealing the truth at the wrong time can backfire. Wield knowledge wisely and understand that truth, while essential, does not always guarantee advantage. Discretion and strategic thinking often hold more power than blunt honesty. Sometimes, the right move is not in what you say, but in what you choose to hold back.

We are taught to seek truth. We are taught to honor it, defend it, and speak it without hesitation. And yet, life—complex, nuanced, layered—rarely rewards truth in its rawest form. The truth is not always a weapon or a shield. Sometimes, it is a weight. Sometimes, it is a spark that, when mishandled, ignites unintended fires.

Knowing the truth does not always offer you the upper hand. In some moments, it can even be a liability.

This isn't a call to abandon truth, but rather a challenge to mature our relationship with it. To realize that having knowledge does not always mean sharing it. That truth, while inherently powerful, is not inherently strategic. It must be wielded with care, timing, and understanding. There are times when truth needs silence to preserve its strength—moments when sharing it may cause more harm than good, not because it is wrong, but because the world around it is not ready for it.

Caution, then, becomes a discipline. It is not fear; it is foresight. It is the practice of knowing when to speak and when to listen, when to expose and when to withhold. It is not about deception, but about discernment—recognizing that power is not only in what you say, but in what you choose not to say.

Strategic restraint is not weakness; it is wisdom in motion. In a world where voices clamor to be heard, where the urge to be right often drowns out the need to be wise, caution reminds us that truth, while noble, is not always tactical. Words once spoken cannot be taken back. And truths revealed without context can become misunderstood weapons.

So, tread carefully—not because the truth is unworthy, but because it is. Honor it enough to protect it. Respect it enough to deliver it only when the impact will match its intent. And never forget: power is not just in knowing the truth—it's in knowing what to do with it.

VALUE

Time is the most valuable currency on the planet; take care not to go bankrupt.

Unlike money, time cannot be earned back once spent. The irreplaceable nature of time urges us to use it wisely. Every moment invested in learning, relationships, and self-growth compounds into a richer life, while wasted time leads to regret. Being mindful of how we allocate our time ensures that we build a life filled with purpose and fulfillment. Just as financial responsibility is essential for wealth, time management is crucial for a well-lived life.

You can borrow money. You can recover from loss. You can rebuild wealth. But no one has ever reclaimed a single second once it has passed. Time is life's most valuable—and most misunderstood—currency. We spend it casually, often unaware that with each tick of the clock, we are drawing from a limited, nonrenewable balance. And yet, we rarely calculate its cost.

Time is the most valuable currency on the planet; take care not to go bankrupt.

The bankruptcy of time is not marked by an empty account but by a full life left unfulfilled—by dreams deferred, relationships neglected, or quiet ambitions silenced by distractions and delay. Consider how we treat money. We budget. We plan. We track every dollar, ensure returns, and guard against waste. What if we treated time with the same respect? What if every hour spent was viewed as an investment—with intentionality, purpose, and a sense of return?

Because time does give returns—but only when spent wisely. Investing it into relationships yields connection. Investing it in growth leads to opportunity. Investing it in service fosters legacy. Every minute you give to something meaningful compounds like interest—quietly but powerfully—into a life of depth and substance. But time wasted? It doesn't just vanish. It becomes regret. Moments missed become memories that never existed. Idle days become empty years. And without realizing it, we wake up to a life built by default, not design. Value isn't about doing more—it's about doing what matters. It's about being present in conversations, focused in your work, intentional in your rest, and protective of your yes. Because your calendar is not just a schedule; it's a reflection of your values.

So ask yourself regularly: Is this how I want to spend my life? Because that's exactly what you're doing. Guard your time the way you would guard your last dollar—because unlike money, you can't earn more of it. Spend it wisely. Invest it deeply. Live as though it's your most precious asset—because it is.

CHOICE

**We don't get to pick our family, but we get to choose
our relationships; choose wisely my friend.**

While family is given to us by birth, the relationships we cultivate are a reflection of our choices. Surround yourself with
people who uplift, support, and challenge you to be better. A strong
circle of meaningful relationships is built on trust, respect, and shared
values. Choosing who we invest our energy in is one of the most powerful decisions we make in life. Be selective, for the right relationships
can elevate your journey, while the wrong ones can drain your spirit.

You are not entirely in control of where you start—but you are
responsible for where you go. Life gifts us with family by default,
but it is through intention that we build connection, belonging,
and love. Relationships—true, chosen, and nurtured—are among the
most powerful forces shaping the course of our lives. And they are all
the result of choice.

We don't get to pick our family, but we get to choose our relationships. That choice is both a freedom and a responsibility.

Every time you open your heart, your time, your energy to someone, you are making an investment. And like all investments, the returns vary. Some relationships give life. They strengthen us, inspire us, hold us accountable, and believe in us when we forget how. Others do the opposite—they drain, manipulate, or diminish. The difference isn't always obvious at first. But over time, every connection either elevates you or anchors you.

That's why choosing your relationships is one of the most important decisions you'll ever make. Not just romantically, but in friendships, partnerships, mentors, and even professional circles. Who you surround yourself with directly influences your mindset, habits, confidence, and growth. It's easy to fall into relationships by convenience, history, or fear of loneliness. But convenience doesn't equate to alignment. Proximity doesn't always mean connection. And history isn't always a reason to keep someone in your life. You have permission to choose differently.

Choose people who push you to become more—not less. Who love you fully, not conditionally. Who respect your boundaries, your growth, your dreams. Choose those whose presence feels like peace, and whose absence reminds you of their value—not their weight. This doesn't mean severing ties with everyone who challenges you. But it does mean being honest about who adds value to your life and who silently subtracts from it. It means recognizing that every relationship is an energy exchange, and your energy is sacred.

So choose wisely, my friend. Not because you're better than anyone else—but because your life, your peace, and your future depend on the people you allow to influence it.

RESILIENCE

Remember your fate and hold strong when faced with dark days.

L ife will throw hardships our way, but resilience is what keeps us moving forward. Challenges are inevitable, but they do not define us—our response to them does. Dark days test our strength, but by holding firm to our purpose and fate, we find the courage to push through adversity. Each struggle is temporary, and perseverance leads to transformation. In the face of storms, stand strong, for resilience is the foundation of all success.

There will be days when the sky feels heavy, when the weight of your past presses on your chest, and when forward seems like a direction for someone stronger, better, more prepared. These are the dark days—the seasons where life stops asking and starts demanding. And yet, it is in these very moments that resilience earns its name. Resilience is not denial. It's not pretending everything is fine. It's the ability to stand firm in the face of everything that says you should crumble. It's the grit to keep going—not because the road is easy, but because your spirit has chosen not to quit.

Remember your fate. That means remember who you are, what you're called to do, and who you're becoming.

Fate doesn't guarantee ease, but it gives purpose to pain. Holding strong in dark days doesn't just protect your future—it builds it. Each act of perseverance adds depth to your character and sharpens your vision. And make no mistake—challenges will come. Sometimes they will arrive without warning, in waves too big to prepare for. But your power lies not in predicting the storm, but in weathering it. In knowing that the wind may bend you, but it will not break you. Because deep beneath the surface, your roots—your values, your vision, your belief in who you're becoming—run deep.

Resilience is a decision repeated. It's choosing to show up one more time. It's finding the strength to speak hope when silence feels safer. It's trusting that transformation is on the other side of trial. You don't need to be unshakable to be resilient. You just need to stay standing. Or crawling. Or inching forward. Even when the world is dark and your soul is tired, forward is still a direction—and resilience is the reason you can keep going.

So when the dark days come, don't question your worth. Don't doubt your destiny. Remember your fate, and hold strong. The storm will pass. And when it does, you'll still be standing. Not just because you endured—but because you chose to.

GENEROSITY

Give freely to the needy and watch your wealth grow.

True wealth is not measured in what we keep but in what we give. Generosity creates abundance—not just in material wealth, but in fulfillment and connection. When we give selflessly, we build a legacy of kindness, and the goodwill we spread often returns to us in ways we never expect. Giving does not diminish our resources; rather, it enriches our lives and strengthens our communities. The act of generosity is an investment in humanity, and its returns are infinite.

There is a strange and beautiful paradox in generosity: the more you give away, the more you possess. We often associate wealth with accumulation—of dollars, things, achievements. But true wealth, the kind that transcends bank accounts and social status, is rooted in what you give away: time, attention, compassion, wisdom, presence. Generosity is the quiet force that builds bridges, softens hearts, and elevates both the giver and the receiver.

Give freely to the needy and watch your wealth grow. Not because giving is a transaction, but because it's a transformation.

Every act of generosity is an expression of belief in abundance—not just of resources, but of spirit. It says, There is enough to share. I am enough to give. The world is better when we lift each other up. Generosity isn't always grand. Sometimes it's as simple as listening. As small as holding a door, offering encouragement, or showing up when it's inconvenient. These moments seem insignificant, but they multiply in impact. What you offer might be the very thing someone else needs to keep going.

And here's the secret: the act of giving changes you. It removes the grip of scarcity. It dismantles selfishness. It invites you to be part of something bigger than yourself. Giving doesn't deplete—it refines. It draws out empathy, humility, and grace. It reminds us that what we do for others often becomes what defines us most. Yes, generosity can take the form of money. But its truest power lies in offering what cannot be measured: your time, your energy, your story, your light. The legacy of your generosity will live in the lives you touched, the dignity you restored, the hope you sparked.

So give. Give without calculating the return. Give without conditions. Give when it's easy, and especially when it's not. Because in that giving, you'll discover the kind of wealth no vault can hold and no thief can take—the wealth of a full heart, a clear conscience, and a life that mattered deeply to others.

ACTION

There are two sets of people in this world: the takers and the doers; you are welcome to pick a side.

Life is shaped by those who take action and those who remain passive. Be among the doers—the people who step up, take risks, and create change. Takers wait for opportunities, while doers seize them. Progress belongs to those who act, not those who merely observe. In every challenge, we have a choice: to stand on the sidelines or to engage fully. The side we pick defines our journey and ultimately, our legacy. Every day, we are offered a simple, quiet choice: to participate or to spectate. And though the choice may seem small in the moment, it has a powerful cumulative effect—shaping our outcomes, our reputation, and the footprint we leave behind.

There are two sets of people in this world: the takers and the doers. One takes from life—waiting for the ideal conditions, hoping to benefit from someone else's initiative. The other gives to life—bringing effort, intention, and initiative to the table. One stands by. The other shows up. This isn't just about being busy. It's about being engaged. Action isn't motion for motion's sake—it's movement with purpose. Doers aren't always the loudest, the most visible, or the most celebrated. But they are the ones who refuse to be defined by indecision. They say yes to effort. Yes to discomfort. Yes to risk. Because they know that inaction guarantees nothing, while action opens doors—even if only one inch at a time.

Takers sit in the waiting room of life, hoping something will arrive.

Doers knock on doors. And when those doors don't open, they build their own. Yes, action requires courage. And no, it won't always bring immediate results. But movement—no matter how imperfect—is the catalyst of transformation. Momentum favors the brave. It rewards the ones who start even when they're unsure of the outcome. And that courage to begin? That's what separates a stagnant life from an evolving one. When you're faced with doubt, fear, or the temptation to delay, remember that every great achievement began with a single, imperfect step. That step didn't guarantee success—but it made it possible.

So pick your side. Not just today, but in the moments that test you. In conversations where your voice could make a difference. In projects that feel bigger than your current confidence. In decisions where comfort would be easier, but courage is required. Choose to do. Because while the world waits, progress is made by those who act.

LOGIC

When faced with a tough decision, let go of emotions and channel your logical and strategic powers.

E motions can cloud judgment, especially in high-stakes situations. Logic and strategy should guide difficult decisions. While emotions are valuable, they should not dictate our actions when clarity and reasoning are needed. Approaching challenges with a rational mindset allows us to make sound choices, free from impulsive reactions. Strategic thinking ensures long-term success, as wisdom emerges from careful analysis rather than fleeting emotions. When uncertainty arises, let logic be your compass.

High-pressure situations stir a storm within. Emotions rise quickly—loud, persuasive, and urgent. In those moments, it's easy to react rather than respond, to move from instinct rather than insight. But clarity doesn't live in the chaos of emotion; it thrives in the calm of logic. When faced with a tough decision, let go of emotions and channel your logical and strategic powers. Not because emotions are wrong—but because they are incomplete. Passion, fear, frustration, even hope, are only part of the equation. Logic doesn't override these feelings—it puts them in perspective. Strong decisions are built like structures: grounded in facts, reinforced by reasoning, and shaped by long-term vision. Emotions can be the spark, but logic is the framework. Without it, decisions collapse under the weight of uncertainty or regret.

A rational mind steps back. It doesn't rush. It evaluates. It examines all sides. And in doing so, it transforms impulse into intention.

When we allow logic to lead, we create space between stimulus and response—space where wisdom has room to speak. That space allows us to avoid reacting to the pressure of now at the expense of what matters next. Strategic thinking is not about being unemotional. It's about being deliberate. It's about making decisions that serve your purpose, not just your mood. It's about aligning your actions with your values and your vision—not just with your stress.

Let logic be your compass. Especially when you're angry. Especially when you're uncertain. Especially when you're tempted to do what feels good instead of what is right. In that clarity, you'll find the power to act—not recklessly, but wisely. And wisdom, unlike emotion, will never ask to be taken back.

STRATEGY

A battle is fought with soldiers but won with the mind; clear your thoughts when faced with adversity.

V ictory is not just about strength but about the ability to think ahead. Strategy is essential in overcoming challenges. When faced with adversity, staying calm and thinking critically ensures that actions are deliberate and effective. A sharp mind can outmaneuver brute force, making strategic thinking the key to overcoming any obstacle. Adversity tests more than muscle—it tests the mind. The chaos of a challenge, much like the confusion of battle, can tempt us to rush, to swing without aim, or to move without a plan. But in the midst of conflict, success favors not the strongest, but the most strategic.

A battle is fought with soldiers but won with the mind. True leadership, true progress, and true impact are born from thoughtfulness, not recklessness. The ability to pause, to assess, and to make calculated moves turns struggle into opportunity and transforms effort into outcome. Strategy isn't about being cold or detached—it's about being focused. It's about replacing panic with planning, distraction with discipline. And when adversity strikes, strategy becomes your armor. While others flail in frustration or fold under pressure, you remain centered, because your choices aren't emotional—they're intentional.

Clarity under pressure is a skill. It's earned through self-awareness, reflection, and preparation.

The mind that knows how to breathe through stress, to sort signal from noise, and to anticipate the next move becomes the most dangerous and effective tool on any battlefield—personal, professional, or relational. In moments when brute force fails, when loud voices lose their power, and when rushing leads to ruin, it's strategy that steps in and turns the tide.

So clear your thoughts. Still the emotional static. Think—not to delay action, but to elevate it. The sharpest mind doesn't just see the fight—it sees the field. It doesn't just strike—it studies. It doesn't just endure—it plans to win. In every battle—big or small—your strategy will always be your greatest strength.

PREPAREDNESS

Pick your battles but always plan for war; safety requires vigilance.

Life's greatest challenges often come unannounced. Be selective in your fights but always ready for the unexpected. Preparedness is not about seeking conflict but about ensuring you have the tools and mindset needed to handle it when it arises. By staying vigilant, you protect yourself and position yourself for success. Trouble doesn't schedule an appointment. It doesn't knock politely or give notice. It arrives when it chooses—fast, fierce, and often in the middle of your most peaceful season.

Pick your battles but always plan for war. That's not a call to live in fear—it's a mindset of readiness. It means you don't swing at every provocation, but you also don't assume peace is permanent. Life, in all its unpredictability, rewards those who prepare not just for what they want, but for what might go wrong.

Preparedness is a quiet form of wisdom.

It's being three steps ahead not because you're paranoid, but because you're responsible. It's having a backup plan, not because you expect failure, but because you honor the importance of what's at stake. Whether in your career, your relationships, your health, or your principles—being prepared gives you stability when everything else is shifting. It sharpens your awareness, builds your resilience, and increases your confidence. People who are prepared don't panic; they pivot.

Planning for war doesn't mean living in conflict. It means living with the awareness that life can shift in an instant. It means sharpening your skills, protecting your peace, and cultivating a mindset that doesn't flinch when the unexpected strikes. Vigilance is not about tension; it's about presence. The most prepared people are not rigid—they are alert. They don't run from difficulty, and they don't seek it either. They simply refuse to be caught unaware.

So choose your battles with wisdom. Don't fight everything. But prepare for anything. Because when you're prepared, you don't just survive the war—you set the terms for how it ends.

DIVERSITY

If all ten colleagues have the same thoughts, it's as meaningless as only soliciting one opinion.

P rogress thrives on diverse perspectives. A room filled with identical ideas limits creativity, whereas a variety of viewpoints fosters innovation and growth. True wisdom comes from embracing diversity and listening to voices different from our own. Agreement may feel comfortable, but it rarely creates breakthrough.

If all ten colleagues have the same thoughts, it's as meaningless as only soliciting one opinion. Different faces, identical voices—this is not collaboration. It's repetition. And while it may move things forward quietly, it rarely moves them forward well. Diversity isn't just a buzzword or a demographic goal—it's a source of strength, creativity, and resilience. When everyone around the table thinks the same way, sees the same angles, and draws the same conclusions, the team becomes predictable. Worse, it becomes blind to risk and opportunity alike. Real innovation doesn't come from echo chambers. It comes from challenge. From friction. From people who respectfully disrupt the groupthink and ask, What if we tried it this way?

To embrace diversity is to welcome perspectives formed by different experiences, cultures, values, and worldviews.

It's to recognize that the best solutions are rarely born from a single story. They emerge from the intersection of many—sometimes clashing, sometimes harmonizing—but always expanding what's possible. And diversity goes beyond surface traits. It includes how people approach problems, what assumptions they question, and how willing they are to speak a truth that others may avoid. It's about cognitive stretch—not conformity. This isn't always easy. Diversity can be messy. It requires humility. It means listening more than defending. It means allowing your ideas to be challenged, and sometimes replaced, by something better. But the reward is worth it. When you cultivate diversity, you don't just get a team—you get a think tank. You don't just protect against bias—you build toward brilliance.

So look around your table. Look at your circle. Look at your systems. Are you surrounded by sameness? Or are you intentionally seeking perspectives that disrupt your comfort but sharpen your clarity? Because progress needs more than agreement. It needs perspective. And perspective starts with listening to someone who doesn't see the world the same way you do.

INSPIRATION

Encourage your family to become the best versions of themselves, friends, strangers, and enemies.

True leadership is about uplifting others. Inspiration is not just for those closest to us but for everyone we encounter. Encouraging growth in those around us creates a ripple effect that extends beyond our immediate circles, ultimately making the world a better place. The true measure of your impact isn't found in your achievements—it's found in who grows because of your presence.

Encourage your family to become the best versions of themselves, friends, strangers, and enemies. Inspiration is not a gift reserved for the few—it is a responsibility shared by all. And when we choose to carry that responsibility with grace, we become catalysts for change in lives far beyond our own. Leadership doesn't always come from a podium. Sometimes, it's the quiet act of believing in someone before they believe in themselves. It's in choosing to see potential when others see only flaws. When we inspire, we hand someone a mirror that shows not just who they are—but who they could be.

This begins at home, but it doesn't end there. It extends to colleagues, strangers in line, even those who oppose us. Because when we lead with inspiration, we choose not to react to people based on how they treat us—but on how we believe they're capable of becoming.

To inspire someone is to speak life into their possibilities.

To uplift them is to show them that transformation is possible, even if they don't see the path yet. Inspiration isn't reserved for the charismatic or the celebrated. It lives in everyday people who choose to show up with intention, encouragement, and integrity. When you live inspired, you give others permission to do the same. And the ripple? It starts with one small gesture—but it doesn't stop there. It travels through families, communities, and generations.

So let your words build. Let your actions inspire. Let your belief in others light a spark that outlives you. Because the greatest legacy isn't what you leave behind—it's who you lift along the way.

PERSPECTIVE

They said words matter, and the word darkness got the shortest end of the stick. What if you were told darkness was tranquil, peaceful, and beautiful?

Perception shapes reality. We are challenged to see things from different angles and to question societal narratives. What we fear or dismiss might hold hidden beauty if we choose to look at it differently. Darkness is rarely given the benefit of the doubt. From childhood, we're taught that darkness means danger, that it's the absence of good, the home of the unknown, the symbol of fear. But what if that's only half the truth?

They said words matter, and the word darkness got the shortest end of the stick. We've judged it by tradition, not by experience. But step outside on a quiet night, away from noise, away from light, and you may find that darkness is not hostile—it's healing. Perspective is the lens through which reality takes shape. And sometimes, to grow, we must be willing to change the lens.

What we fear might be misunderstood. What we avoid may be exactly what we need. Darkness, after all, brings rest. It brings stillness. It reveals stars you can't see in daylight. It doesn't always conceal—it invites reflection, it calls for presence, it forces us to listen more deeply.

Perspective allows us to rewrite the narratives we've been handed.

It gives us the freedom to reclaim what we were taught to fear and ask, Is this really the enemy? Or is it just unfamiliar? This shift in perception isn't about being naïve—it's about being open. It's about honoring the complexity of things we once labeled too quickly. When we shift our view, we unlock new meaning. And with that meaning comes empathy, creativity, and growth.

So next time you encounter darkness—literal or metaphorical—pause before you judge it. Sit with it. Learn from it. Because what we fear often holds the lesson we need most.

ADAPTABILITY

Get comfortable being uncomfortable when success is waiting around the corner.

Growth begins where comfort ends. The path to success is often lined with discomfort, uncertainty, and challenge. Those who are willing to adapt—to embrace the unknown—gain access to opportunities that others miss. Success rarely arrives in predictable packages; it demands flexibility, resilience, and the courage to keep moving through unfamiliar territory. The more you practice being adaptable, the more you position yourself for breakthroughs just beyond the edge of your comfort zone.

Comfort zones feel safe—but they are rarely where transformation happens. Get comfortable being uncomfortable when success is waiting around the corner. That discomfort you feel when you're stretching, adjusting, or stepping into the unknown? That's the signal you're getting closer to something important.

Adaptability is not a passive trait—it's an active decision to remain flexible when life bends your expectations.

It's a mindset that doesn't crumble under pressure, but reshapes under it. When plans change, adaptable people shift. When adversity strikes, they find new ways forward. Success often demands more than talent or timing—it demands movement. It requires the willingness to pivot, to learn, and to evolve without the guarantee of immediate results. Adaptability means being anchored by your purpose, not your preferences. It means holding your vision, but letting go of how you thought you'd get there.

Many miss opportunities because they don't recognize them in their discomfort. They expect doors to look polished, predictable, and aligned with their current skills. But most breakthroughs don't arrive that way. They come wrapped in change. They come disguised as setbacks. They come when we least feel ready. And that's the point. The more you practice adaptability, the more agile your mindset becomes. What once shook you becomes your new baseline. What once felt impossible becomes a challenge worth accepting.

So embrace the stretch. Trust the shift. Welcome the discomfort. Because that's where growth lives.

DISCIPLINE

The art of discipline is more mental than physical; focusing on your mental battles will help defeat your physical encounters.

Discipline is not about brute strength—it's about mental mastery. The toughest battles are often internal: overcoming doubt, resisting temptation, and staying focused when distractions loom. Once the mind is trained, the body follows. Building discipline requires consistency, not perfection, and it begins with mastering the small choices each day. The more control you gain over your thoughts, the more power you'll have over your actions—and your outcomes.

Discipline doesn't begin in the body—it begins in the mind. The art of discipline is more mental than physical. You can have all the tools, the resources, the routines—but if your mindset isn't sharp, everything else crumbles under pressure. Discipline is about delayed gratification. It's choosing the harder right over the easier wrong. It's resisting the urge to quit when no one is watching. It's reminding yourself of your "why" when everything in you wants to retreat to what's familiar.

The physical expression of discipline—waking up early, working out, doing the hard things—is fueled by a deeper internal battle. That battle happens in the quiet moments: when the alarm rings, when temptation whispers, when distractions flood in. If you win in your head, your actions will follow. Mental strength is built just like physical strength—through repetition. Through showing up, again and again, even when motivation is gone. Through building habits that override emotion. Through learning to be comfortable with discomfort.

Discipline doesn't require perfection. It requires commitment.

You will stumble. You will slip. But discipline picks you up faster. It shortens the gap between failure and forward motion. And the more you train your mind to obey your values instead of your feelings, the more freedom you gain. Freedom from regret. Freedom from inconsistency. Freedom from the chaos of living by impulse.

So take control of your thoughts. They're not just passing notions—they are the architects of your life. When your mind is strong, your actions follow. And when your actions align with your purpose, anything is possible.

COURAGE

When self-preservation defeats self-courage, our world has lost its moral compass.

True courage is not the absence of fear—it's the decision to act despite it. When we prioritize personal comfort over doing what is right, society begins to falter. Courage is the backbone of integrity and justice. It calls us to step forward when it's easier to remain silent. The moral compass of the world is maintained by individuals willing to take risks for the sake of truth, fairness, and others.

Comfort is easy. Courage is not. When self-preservation defeats self-courage, our world has lost its moral compass. The moment we choose safety over principle—when silence becomes easier than truth—we begin to lose something far more valuable than comfort: our integrity.

Courage is rarely loud. It often takes place in small moments: speaking up when it's unpopular, standing firm when it's costly, doing what's right when the crowd does what's easy. It is the quiet decision to step forward—not because fear isn't present, but because something greater is at stake.

Fear is natural. Courage is a choice.

And it's a choice we must make repeatedly. When we withhold courage in the name of self-preservation, we shrink not only our voice but our impact. The people who shift the world are not those who are fearless—but those who act in spite of it. They are the whistleblowers, the protectors, the bridge-builders, the truth-tellers.

Courage asks you to trade your silence for significance. It is the engine behind justice, the fuel behind progress, and the shield of those who protect the vulnerable. It takes courage to be kind in a world that can be cruel. It takes courage to forgive when bitterness feels justified. It takes courage to rise again after failure, to apologize, to change, to lead. And every time you answer the call to courage, the world tilts back toward balance.

So when you feel afraid, when you are tempted to look away, remember: someone else is waiting for the permission your courage will give them. Be the one who steps forward.

Persistence

The law of numbers: 1000 thoughts, 100 requests, 10 opportunities for 1 success; never give up.

Success is often a numbers game. Many efforts may lead to few rewards—but that one reward can be life-changing. Behind every success story are countless failures and rejections. The key is to keep going. Persistence wears down obstacles and reveals new pathways. The only sure way to fail is to quit before the breakthrough comes. Most people give up too soon.

The law of numbers: 1000 thoughts, 100 requests, 10 opportunities for 1 success; never give up. This is not discouragement—it's reality. And it's also the foundation of every major breakthrough the world has ever known. Persistence is the ability to show up when the results haven't. It's knocking on doors that may not open—until one does. It's sending one more message, making one more attempt, learning one more lesson when it would be easier to walk away.

You're not losing because you've failed—you're only losing if you stop trying.

Behind every celebrated story is a trail of rejection letters, missed calls, and moments of self-doubt. But the ones who succeed are the ones who keep going—not because it's easy, but because they've decided that their vision is worth the effort. Every attempt sharpens your skill. Every "no" brings you closer to a "yes." Every setback is preparing you for something greater than the moment you're in.

Persistence isn't about ignoring obstacles—it's about refusing to be defined by them. It's doing the work even when no one sees it. It's believing in the value of your pursuit when others don't. It's pressing forward not because success is guaranteed—but because quitting guarantees failure.

So keep moving. Keep pushing. Keep building. Your breakthrough may be closer than you think. And when it arrives, it will make every failed attempt worth it.

MINDFULNESS

Cherish your time and be mindful not to waste it on those who find no value in such treasure.

Time is the one resource we never get back. Be intentional about where you invest your energy. Mindfulness means more than presence—it's about knowing what and who deserves your time. When people take your time for granted, they take a piece of your life. Protect it, value it, and share it only with those who understand its worth. Mindfulness is more than breathing exercises and calm spaces—it's about clarity, boundaries, and intention.

Cherish your time and be mindful not to waste it on those who find no value in such treasure. Time is sacred. And every moment you spend is a piece of your life you will never retrieve. This isn't meant to instill fear, but to remind you of the power in your daily choices.

Being mindful means paying attention not only to what you're doing but to why you're doing it—and who you're doing it with. It means asking yourself, "Does this align with who I am and what I value?" before giving your time, your energy, or your peace.

Some people will appreciate your time like sunlight. Others will absorb it like a void.

Your presence is a gift. Your attention is currency. And your time is a limited account that deserves to be spent wisely. When you become intentional about where you focus, who you listen to, and how you show up, you begin to experience life with more depth, more meaning, and more freedom. Mindfulness is the art of living on purpose. It's making sure the pace of your life doesn't outrun the purpose of your life.

So pause. Observe. Choose. And remember that being mindful doesn't mean saying yes to everything—it means saying yes only to what truly matters.

RESISTANCE

When you give in to pain, fear, and thoughts, failure finds its way into your home.

Pain, fear, and doubt are inevitable—but surrendering to them invites defeat. Resist giving in to mental and emotional obstacles. The strength to succeed lies in resilience, in standing firm when your inner voice tells you to stop. Resistance is a discipline, a habit, a shield against collapse. Every time you fight through discomfort, you reinforce your capacity to win.

Pain shows up without invitation. Fear whispers when you least expect it. Doubt finds the cracks and creeps in slowly. These forces are not signs that something is wrong—they are proof that something is at stake. When you give in to pain, fear, and thoughts, failure finds its way into your home. But giving in is not the same as feeling. You will feel it all. You're supposed to. The key is not letting it own you.

Resistance is not about pretending you're unshaken. It's about choosing to keep standing even when you are.

It's about confronting the storm with resolve—not because you're unafraid, but because something in you is louder than your fear. We often imagine resistance as this heroic, all-or-nothing moment. But in truth, it's often quiet. It's the decision to show up for yourself when no one's watching. It's taking one more step when you're already exhausted. It's saying, not today to the part of your mind that begs for an easier route.

Every time you resist the temptation to quit, every time you push back against the negative voice in your head, you're building something unshakable. You're reinforcing your inner architecture. And over time, those small acts of defiance become the foundation of strength. Resistance is a practice. A mindset. A promise to yourself that no matter how heavy the burden, no matter how fierce the fear, you will not surrender.

So when discomfort rises, meet it with discipline. When fear roars, answer with stillness. And when doubt knocks, let it know: failure may threaten your doorstep, but it will never find a home within you.

INTEGRITY

Hold yourself to a higher standard than others and never fall short of the scrutiny of "the mob."

I ntegrity means doing what's right even when no one is watching—and especially when everyone is. Be your own harshest critic. Hold the line even under pressure from the crowd. Popular opinion changes with the wind, but personal standards anchored in truth remain unshaken. When you live with integrity, external scrutiny loses its power.

The loudest voices in the room are not always the most principled. Hold yourself to a higher standard than others and never fall short of the scrutiny of "the mob." Because the mob will cheer for you today and condemn you tomorrow. Their approval is fickle, but your conscience is constant.

Integrity isn't about applause—it's about alignment.

It's about living in such a way that your actions don't need explanation and your decisions don't need an audience. It's choosing right over easy, principle over popularity, and truth over trend—even when it costs you something. The world constantly shifts its definition of right and wrong. What's celebrated today may be canceled tomorrow. But when you're anchored in integrity, you don't have to keep up—you just have to stand firm. You become the kind of person who doesn't flinch in the face of scrutiny because you've already held yourself to a higher bar behind closed doors.

This is not about arrogance. It's about discipline. It's about living in such a way that you never have to look over your shoulder. When you make decisions guided by inner values rather than external validation, you strip the crowd of its power over you.

Integrity is forged in private but tested in public. When pressure mounts, when compromise feels easier, and when silence feels safer, that's when character is revealed. Will you bend for comfort? Or will you stand for something more?

You don't need to be perfect to walk in integrity. You just need to be honest, consistent, and committed to holding your own line—even if no one else does. Let your standard be yours, not theirs. And let your truth speak—especially when the crowd goes quiet.

FREEDOM

Give me safety and love, but please don't take my freedom away.

Safety and love are comforts of life, but freedom is its essence. The human spirit yearns for autonomy. Freedom allows us to think, to speak, to choose—without it, the soul is confined, even in luxury. A life of comfort without freedom is a life half-lived. To protect your freedom is to protect your identity, your purpose, and your future.

Safety can shelter you. Love can fulfill you. But only freedom can let you become who you were truly meant to be. Give me safety and love, but please don't take my freedom away. It's a quiet plea with thunderous meaning: without freedom, everything else becomes conditional. Comfort without autonomy is a gilded cage. Even peace becomes hollow if it is forced.

**Freedom is more than the ability to roam—it is
the ability to choose.**

To choose your words, your beliefs, your path, your purpose. When those choices are taken from you, even the most luxurious life becomes a prison. The human spirit was not built for confinement. It was designed to stretch, to question, to create, to evolve. That spirit shrinks under oppression—not always physical, but emotional, mental, and ideological. And once freedom is compromised, even love feels limited, even safety feels suffocating.

But freedom is fragile. It must be guarded, not just in our societies, but in our relationships, in our thoughts, and in our daily choices. Sometimes, the threat doesn't come from force—it comes from comfort. From slowly giving up our voice to fit in. From staying quiet to avoid conflict. From shrinking to keep the peace. To be free is to own your truth without apology. To speak it, to live it, and to defend it—not at the expense of others, but never at the cost of yourself.

So fight for love. Fight for safety. But above all, fight to remain free. Because when freedom dies, everything else loses its meaning.

RISK

The goat on the cliff's edge remains oblivious to risk, not because it doesn't exist but because it learned to live with it.

R isk is part of every meaningful pursuit. Like the goat navigating the cliff, we must learn to live with uncertainty. It's not about ignoring danger but becoming skilled in handling it. Mastery comes with familiarity. The more we engage with risk, the less it controls us—and the more capable we become of achieving great heights. High ground always offers the best view—but it comes with steep edges.

The goat on the cliff's edge remains oblivious to risk, not because it doesn't exist, but because it learned to live with it.

That's not naivety—it's skill. Mastery. Familiarity earned through experience, built one careful step at a time. We often think of risk as something to avoid. But the truth is, risk is the toll for crossing into any meaningful territory. It lives in every job change, every love pursued, every dream chased, every truth told. Risk surrounds anything that matters. But fear doesn't mean stop. It means pay attention.

The ones who thrive are not those who avoid risk altogether—they're the ones who stop letting it paralyze them. They've trained themselves to feel fear without being ruled by it. They've learned to assess risk, prepare for it, and move forward anyway. Growth doesn't come from staying in the safe zone. The cliff may be narrow, but it also offers a view of what's possible.

You won't eliminate risk—not fully. But you can walk beside it with clarity, self-trust, and courage. Every step forward, every moment you lean into discomfort, you shrink fear's power and grow your own. Because at some point, the risk of standing still becomes greater than the risk of stepping forward. And when you get to that edge, remember: you're not falling. You're learning how to climb higher.

NECESSITY

**Food remains an essential part of life; the same holds
true for the power of sleep.**

We often acknowledge the importance of food but overlook
rest as a fundamental necessity. Sleep is not a luxury—it is
vital to our well-being, clarity, and emotional health. Just as hunger
weakens the body, exhaustion drains the mind and spirit. Balance
begins with honoring both our physical and mental needs. Fuel your
body and restore your soul with rest. We know to eat when we're
hungry, but we ignore the yawn. We caffeinate through exhaustion.

We wear fatigue like a badge of honor.

And we call it productivity. Food remains an essential part of life;
the same holds true for the power of sleep. But unlike hunger, sleep
deprivation doesn't always alert us with a growl. It creeps in quiet-

ly—clouding our thinking, dulling our emotions, eroding our creativity and resilience.

Rest isn't a reward for working hard—it's the fuel that makes the work possible. Sleep is a reset, not a weakness. It's how the mind reboots, how memory is consolidated, how clarity is restored, and how emotional well-being is protected.

We talk about mental health, about performance, about high output. Yet too often, we sacrifice rest in the name of achievement—unaware that we are dulling the very edge we need to cut through our goals. We need to recalibrate our definition of strength. Rest is not retreat. It's reinforcement. When you rest with intention, you sharpen your focus, increase your capacity, and build sustainable energy.

So eat well, yes. Feed your body. But also, rest well. Sleep deeply. Unplug. Reflect. Reclaim your rhythm. Because no matter how ambitious you are, if you don't rest, you break.

LEGACY

What good is knowledge held captive by another; pass on life's greatest gift to the next generation.

Knowledge becomes powerful only when it is shared. Leaving a legacy isn't about possessions—it's about wisdom and experience. The most enduring impact we can make is to teach, guide, and uplift others. A life well-lived echoes through generations when we choose to give back what we've learned.

Legacy is not built in grand gestures—it's etched into moments, conversations, decisions, and stories. What good is knowledge held captive by another; pass on life's greatest gift to the next generation. Wisdom that dies with you helps no one. Experience that stays locked inside becomes weight, not worth.

You don't have to be famous to leave a legacy. You just have to live with intention. You have to give away what life has taught you—the truths you bled for, the mistakes you grew from, the insights earned through trial and time. Think of all the times someone's words, actions, or example shaped you. They may not even know the impact they made. But it mattered. And so will yours.

**Share your knowledge. Teach those around you.
Speak life into younger voices.**

Tell your stories—the real ones. Not the polished versions, but the honest ones. Let others see your path, not just your position. The impact multiplies. One story shared becomes a mindset changed. One lesson passed down becomes a mistake avoided. One act of guidance becomes a ripple that outlives you. That's legacy. Not what you leave for others, but what you leave in them.

CHANGE

Don't fear the future; embracing change is a human's long-lasting tradition.

C hange is the only constant in life, and humanity has always adapted. Resistance to change only delays progress. While the future is uncertain, our ability to grow through it is time-tested. Embracing change with curiosity and courage turns challenges into opportunities and fear into freedom. Adaptation is not just a survival tool—it's a legacy written into our DNA.

Don't fear the future; embracing change is a human's long-lasting tradition. From the earliest migrations to modern innovations, human history is a series of transitions—each one propelled by uncertainty and met with resilience. We are wired to evolve. To outgrow what no longer serves us. To step into the unfamiliar, even if our first instinct is to resist it.

Change shakes foundations. It interrupts routines. It redefines the comfortable. But it also creates the soil in which possibility takes root.

Without change, there is no innovation, no discovery, no personal evolution. Everything that grows must first let go of what it once was.

Fear of change is natural—but it must not become a way of life.

When we cling to the past simply because it is familiar, we trade potential for predictability. We shrink our lives to fit old versions of ourselves. But when we meet change with curiosity—when we ask, What can this teach me? Where can this lead me?—we transform fear into freedom. We give ourselves permission to become more. Change doesn't always come gently. It often arrives disguised as disruption. But even then, it is a catalyst—pushing us toward who we are becoming, not punishing who we were.

So walk into the future not with resistance, but with readiness. You've done this before. You've adapted, grown, stretched, and survived. You'll do it again.

EMPATHY

When we forget to look back to aid those we left behind, it leaves a lasting scar on tomorrow's civilization.

Empathy is the thread that binds humanity together. We are called to extend our hands, not just forward but backward—to uplift those still climbing. Progress without compassion is hollow. Our legacy will not only be measured by what we achieved, but by who we helped along the way.

We are not meant to run ahead alone. When we forget to look back to aid those we left behind, it leaves a lasting scar on tomorrow's civilization. Advancement is meaningless if it comes at the cost of compassion. Progress must not be measured only by how far we've gone, but by how many we've brought with us.

Empathy is more than feeling—it is action.

It is the conscious choice to see others not as obstacles, but as reflections of ourselves in different seasons. It's remembering how it felt to be overlooked, unheard, or left behind—and deciding we won't let others feel the same. In a world that celebrates speed and achievement, empathy asks us to slow down, to look back, and to reach out. It challenges the notion that we must choose between personal success and collective well-being.

You can build. You can rise. But if you forget the hands that once held you up—or ignore the ones now reaching toward you—your success becomes shallow. Empathy is not weakness. It is strength wrapped in compassion. It's choosing to carry more, not because you have to—but because you can. The most powerful people are not those who dominate others, but those who lift others while leading themselves.

So as you climb, look back. As you rise, reach out. The mark you leave on this world will not be in your trophies, but in the lives you helped lift along the way.

HAPPINESS

Happiness has a different meaning to others and is emblematic of our culture.

Happiness is not one-size-fits-all. Joy is shaped by values, beliefs, and lived experiences. What brings contentment to one may not move another. Respecting these differences helps build a more accepting, harmonious world. Seek your own version of happiness, and honor the path of others. We chase happiness as if it comes with universal coordinates. But the truth is, it doesn't live in a single destination—it's deeply personal, wildly varied, and beautifully unique.

Happiness has a different meaning to others and is emblematic of our culture. What brings joy to one person may be invisible to another. Culture, upbringing, personal history, temperament—all shape what happiness looks and feels like. For some, it's the thrill of achievement; for others, it's the quiet of simplicity. For one, it might be celebration; for another, solitude.

Trying to define happiness by someone else's standards is like trying to wear their shoes—they may look good, but they won't take you far.

The goal is not to mimic another's joy, but to discover your own. This discovery takes honesty. It takes permission—to let go of what "should" make you happy, and embrace what actually does. Maybe your happiness isn't glamorous or easily explained. Maybe it's morning coffee alone, or building something with your hands, or protecting your peace in a chaotic world. That's enough.

And as you pursue your own joy, remember that others are doing the same. When you respect their pursuit—even if it's different from yours—you foster empathy. You help build a world that doesn't just tolerate differences but honors them. Because true happiness flourishes not in uniformity, but in authenticity.

So protect your version of joy. Cultivate it. Share it—but don't impose it. And in doing so, give others the space to do the same.

PROGRESS

I crawled yesterday, walked today, and hope to run tomorrow, chasing the shadow of someone I never knew.

Progress is not always linear. This poetic reflection captures the unpredictable nature of growth. Sometimes we sprint, sometimes we stumble—but forward is forward. Whether you're chasing dreams or healing from pain, the movement itself is what matters. The path may not be clear, but the effort carves the way.

Growth doesn't always look like progress. Sometimes, it looks like crawling. I crawled yesterday, walked today, and hope to run tomorrow, chasing the shadow of someone I never knew. This is not just a line—it's a reflection of what it means to evolve. The path to becoming who we're meant to be isn't straight, smooth, or logical. It's filled with stops and starts, doubts and breakthroughs, regressions and leaps forward.

Progress is a spectrum. Some days, you're running with clarity. Other days, you're dragging yourself forward, unsure if it counts.

But it does. Every inch gained, every fear faced, every time you try again—that's movement. Chasing the shadow of someone you never knew means becoming the version of yourself that's always been waiting beneath the surface. The "you" shaped not by what you've done, but by what you're willing to become. It's not about speed or perfection—it's about persistence and direction.

There will be days when you feel behind. But behind what? A timeline you didn't create? A comparison you didn't choose? The truth is, you're not behind—you're on your way. And while your pace may change, your movement matters. Even crawling is progress when you refuse to stop. So keep going. Not because it's easy—but because you're worth the effort.

LOVE

In the chaos where hate and pain emerge, the only defense is love for one another.

Love is our greatest armor against the darkness of the world. In times of turmoil, love—selfless, resilient, and compassionate—restores peace. It is not weakness, but strength of the highest kind. When the world feels like it's unraveling—when hate rises, when pain spreads, when division seems louder than unity—there remains one force powerful enough to stand against it: love.

In the chaos where hate and pain emerge, the only defense is love for one another. Not the kind of love that is passive, fragile, or convenient—but a love that chooses to stand firm in the face of bitterness. A love that reaches past anger. A love that holds the line when everything else falls apart. This kind of love is not soft. It is not blind. It doesn't ignore injustice or excuse harm. Instead, it responds to darkness with defiance. It says, "I will not become what wounded me." It says, "I will not answer hate with more hate."

Love in the face of chaos is a revolutionary act.

It takes strength to be kind when cruelty is easier. It takes courage to see someone's humanity when your pain says otherwise. And it takes radical conviction to believe in healing when the world profits off division. But love is not just a feeling—it's a decision. It's showing up when others turn away. It's holding someone accountable with grace. It's choosing compassion over contempt, even when it's uncomfortable. It's forgiveness that frees you, empathy that bridges gaps, and presence that restores peace.

CONNECTION

While sharing a bench with a stranger, take the opportunity to say hello.

In a world full of disconnection, small gestures matter. A simple greeting can bridge divides, spark stories, and change the course of someone's day. Behind every stranger is a potential friend—and behind every hello is the start of understanding. Connection begins in the smallest moments.

While sharing a bench with a stranger, take the opportunity to say hello. It may seem insignificant, but it holds the potential to shift the energy of two lives. One gesture. One sentence. One smile. That's all it takes. We live in a world where isolation often masquerades as independence. We walk past each other with earbuds in and heads down. We scroll through timelines filled with people, yet feel increasingly alone. But the remedy isn't always grand or complex—it's as simple as presence.

A hello is not just a greeting; it's an invitation.

An invitation to acknowledge someone's existence. To honor their presence. To extend warmth in a world that can feel cold and indifferent. When you speak to someone you don't know, you break the barrier of "otherness." You remind them—and yourself—that we are more alike than we are different.

Connection doesn't always lead to friendship, but it always leaves a trace. It says, You are seen. You are heard. You matter. And in a culture where invisibility is one of the quietest forms of suffering, that matters more than we think. So look up. Smile. Say hello. You never know who's waiting for someone to notice them. And you never know when that someone might be you.

HUMANITY

Kudos to the commoner who saved countless lives with a smile and a gesture and continued a journey of thankless healing.

The greatest acts of service often go unnoticed. Unsung heroes—everyday people whose kindness and care create real impact—may never receive recognition, but their influence ripples far and wide. In quiet moments of compassion, the true essence of humanity shines. Greatness is not always loud.

Kudos to the commoner who saved countless lives with a smile and a gesture and continued a journey of thankless healing. Not because they sought recognition—but because their heart couldn't turn away. The world celebrates achievements, awards, and accolades. But the soul of humanity is often found in the uncelebrated—the nurse who stays after her shift to sit with a patient. The neighbor who checks in during a storm. The stranger who offers kindness without agenda.

These are not acts for headlines. These are acts that hold the world together.

True humanity lives in quiet sacrifice. In doing good with no expectation of applause.

In understanding that healing doesn't require a platform—it requires presence. Every small, unnoticed gesture becomes a thread in the larger fabric of collective care. The commoner, the healer, the giver—they are the foundation of communities, the keepers of hope. Their impact is not measured in trophies, but in trust. Not in awards, but in the lives they touch. And though they walk paths of humility, their footprints are heavy with purpose.

So if your work goes unseen, if your efforts are unacknowledged, don't lose heart. What you do in quiet still echoes. And you may never know how deeply your humanity changed someone else's world.

BRAVERY

We salute those who bravely save the day when gold, silver, cash, and power are worthless in the face of tyranny.

True bravery rises in the face of danger without the promise of reward. Those who act not for recognition or gain, but because it is the right thing to do, uphold justice when it matters most. When society is tested, it's not wealth or influence that saves us—it's the courage of the few who choose justice over fear. These are the quiet heroes who remind us what real valor looks like.

Courage wears no uniform. It's not always on display. Often, it moves quietly, unnoticed, beneath the noise of wealth and power. We salute those who bravely save the day when gold, silver, cash, and power are worthless in the face of tyranny. When comfort collapses and chaos rises, it is not privilege that shields us—but principle. Not riches that redeem us—but resolve.

Bravery is the moment someone chooses what's right over what's easy.

It's found in the firefighter running into flames, the protester standing in silence, the teacher shielding a child, the doctor refusing to turn away. It's action without audience, sacrifice without applause. True bravery does not seek glory. It is fueled by a sense of duty—a moral clarity that says, Even if it costs me, I must act. These brave souls show up not for the recognition, but because their conscience leaves them no other choice. They are the defenders of dignity, the frontline of justice. And though their names may not be carved into monuments, their impact is etched into the fabric of freedom.

Let us not reserve honor only for those who win. Let us honor those who stand when others fold, who protect when others flee, who give when others take. Because in a world that often idolizes wealth and celebrity, bravery reminds us what truly holds value.

Appreciation

Hail to the sun, missed in the night's embrace and longed for on cloudy days; we promise to withhold judgment on those hot, beautiful summer days.

Appreciation is a poetic reminder of how often we take life's blessings for granted. We miss the sun when it's gone, yet complain when it blazes overhead. Recognizing value in the moment—not just in its absence—teaches us gratitude. When we learn to be grateful—even for discomfort—we open the door to a more peaceful and grounded existence. The sun rises every day, and yet it is only in its absence that we remember its warmth.

Hail to the sun, missed in the night's embrace and longed for on cloudy days; we promise to withhold judgment on those hot, beautiful summer days. Appreciation is not about dramatic gestures—it's about recognition. A quiet awareness that what we have now is enough, even if it's not perfect. We live much of life in hindsight. We understand joy best in its absence, comfort when it's gone, and connection when it's broken. But what if we chose instead to live in real-time recognition? To feel the value of a moment while we're still in it?

Gratitude doesn't require perfection—it requires presence.

Appreciation shifts how we see the world. It turns inconveniences into opportunities. It teaches us to honor even the discomfort, because the heat of a summer day is still a blessing to someone longing for light. To appreciate is to pay attention. To pause and say, This matters. This is. This is good. This is enough. Let us practice appreciation not just for what we long for, but for what is already here. And in doing so, we'll learn that peace doesn't come from more—it comes from recognizing what we already have.

NATURE

The best air purifier is still Mother Nature with her beautiful, majestic forest.

Modern solutions pale in comparison to nature's design. Forests are more than scenery—they are healers, protectors, and providers. In their silence, they cleanse the air, nourish the earth, and calm the mind. Respect for nature is not just an environmental stance—it's a return to balance and wisdom. Mother Nature doesn't need to be reinvented—she only needs to be remembered.

The best air purifier is still Mother Nature with her beautiful, majestic forest. In a world of rapid technological advancement and engineered efficiency, we often overlook the silent miracles happening in the natural world. While we chase solutions in labs, forests have been quietly purifying, balancing, and healing for millennia.

Nature doesn't need attention to do its work—but it does need protection.

The forest is not just a collection of trees; it's a living, breathing sanctuary. It takes in our waste and gives back clean air. It absorbs our noise and returns stillness. It balances chaos with harmony and movement with silence. In every leaf, every breeze, every patch of filtered light, nature teaches us something about how to live. It reminds us to slow down. To breathe deeper. To observe rather than control.

We spend billions trying to replicate what nature offers freely—yet often, we forget to value it until it's lost. The forest is not a luxury or a backdrop. It's part of us. It reflects the balance we crave, the peace we long for, and the clarity we seek. To reconnect with nature is to reconnect with ourselves. When we walk among the trees, we don't just find fresh air—we find perspective. We find that silence isn't empty. It's full of answers.

So honor the earth. Protect her forests. Not just because they're beautiful—but because they are vital to life, and to the soul.

EXPLORATION

Immerse yourself in the beauty and culture around the globe to stimulate your creative genes.

There is no substitute for lived experience. Step beyond your comfort zone and discover the world's rich diversity. Every culture holds lessons, stories, and ideas waiting to ignite your imagination. Exploration doesn't just open your eyes—it expands your mind and feeds your creativity with the inspiration of the unknown.

You cannot grow in a box. Creativity, empathy, understanding—all expand with exposure. Immerse yourself in the beauty and culture around the globe to stimulate your creative genes. Travel is not just about distance—it's about depth. Exploration isn't about escape. It's about becoming more.

Every place you visit, every culture you engage, adds a new brushstroke to the canvas of your identity.

You begin to see how others live, love, struggle, and celebrate. You realize your way isn't the only way. Your view isn't the full view. This isn't just cultural—it's deeply creative. Ideas live in different geographies, and inspiration thrives in unfamiliar places. When you explore, your imagination stretches. Your assumptions soften. Your vision sharpens.

Exploration also humbles you. It reminds you that the world is vast, and you are part of something beautiful and bigger than your routines. The more you step outside yourself, the more you understand what lies within you. So travel—not only with your feet but with your heart and mind. Listen deeply. Observe gently. Allow wonder to lead you. Because the world is not short on beauty—it's short on people willing to notice. And when you return, you'll carry pieces of the world with you—not as souvenirs, but as lenses to see life more fully.

BEAUTY

Inspiration becomes standard, so beauty lies dormant within us all.

We often search for beauty outside ourselves—through art, people, and landscapes. But beauty is not something to be found, it must be awakened. Inspiration may light the way, but true beauty is internal, quietly waiting to be recognized and nurtured. When we look inward, we uncover a radiant truth: we were always enough. We are surrounded by curated images of beauty—airbrushed faces, filtered lives, and polished expressions of what we've been taught to admire. But beneath all that noise, a quieter truth waits to be heard:

Beauty lies dormant within us all.

It is not reserved for the chosen, the flawless, or the celebrated. It doesn't belong to a specific body type, skin tone, status, or trend. True beauty is not defined by symmetry or shape. It is the expression of your spirit—the raw, radiant light that emerges when you live aligned with your truth. But because inspiration has become constant—accessible at every swipe, scroll, and search—we've become desensitized. We've mistaken the pursuit of aesthetics for the presence of beauty. We compare ourselves to art, forgetting that we are art. We chase standards set by systems and strangers and then wonder why we feel disconnected from ourselves.

Beauty isn't missing. It's just unfound—beneath layers of criticism, comparison, and conditioned belief. It's in the laugh lines earned from joy. The stretch marks carved by life. The eyes that still hold softness despite all they've seen. The resilience to get back up. The ability to feel deeply. To forgive. To speak honestly. To love boldly. And it's in your quiet moments—the ones you don't post. The ones no one applauds. When you give without expecting anything in return. When you show up even when you're tired. When you sit in silence and choose to accept yourself anyway.

The world may not always recognize this beauty. But that doesn't make it any less real. The challenge isn't to find beauty. It's to recognize it—first in yourself, then in others. When you begin to look at yourself through eyes of compassion instead of criticism, you stop trying to meet the standard and start setting it. And the more you awaken that beauty within you, the more you see it everywhere—in broken places, in overlooked people, in imperfect moments. You are not lacking beauty. You are overflowing with it. It's time you believed it.

DEPTH

They claim space offers the depth where no one has gone before until you search one's mind.

Outer space may seem vast, but the mind holds a universe all its own. Explore the richness within yourself and others. Human thought, emotion, and memory are layered and boundless. To understand another's mind—or your own—is to embark on the most intricate voyage of all. The deeper you go, the more you discover. We often look to the stars in search of wonder, imagining galaxies that stretch into the infinite. But the most profound mystery might not be overhead—it might be behind our eyes.

They claim space offers the depth where no one has gone before until you search one's mind. The human mind—your mind—is an uncharted cosmos. Thought, emotion, memory, and experience collide and stretch in directions we have yet to fully comprehend. It is the deepest, most intricate terrain we'll ever explore. We fear going too deep sometimes—not into oceans or outer space—but into ourselves.

We skim the surface of our pain, suppress our questions, and distract from our fears. But depth is where the truth lives. It's where meaning begins. It's where healing hides.

> **To search someone's mind—or your own—is to take a journey with no map, no end point, and no promises.**

But what you gain is understanding. Awareness. Empathy. The surface might feel safe, but it's shallow. Real connection, real transformation, happens in depth—in conversations that go beyond the expected, in silences that ask to be honored, in the willingness to ask yourself, Why do I feel this? Where did this belief begin? What lies beneath this reaction?

The mind is a landscape of both darkness and light, and navigating it takes courage. But it also brings clarity. And the more you explore it, the more capable you become of navigating others—with patience, compassion, and care. Don't be afraid to go inward. Don't be afraid to go deeper. Because everything extraordinary you seek out there already exists inside you—waiting to be discovered.

Self-Care

It's ok to be selfish, primarily when others depend on your ability to maintain your physical and spiritual well-being.

T aking care of yourself isn't indulgence—it's necessity. Self-care is responsibility. When others count on your strength, energy, and clarity, prioritizing your wellness is a gift to everyone you serve. You cannot pour from an empty cup. Protect your peace, nurture your body, and refuel your spirit. You cannot lead from depletion. You cannot love from burnout. You cannot give what you do not have.

It's ok to be selfish, primarily when others depend on your ability to maintain your physical and spiritual well-being. We've been taught to equate self-care with self-indulgence, as if caring for yourself takes something away from others. But the opposite is true: caring for yourself is caring for them.

Self-care is not bubble baths and spa days—though it can be. It's also boundaries.

It's saying no to protect your yes. It's leaving the event early so you can rest. It's stepping back before resentment replaces love. It's knowing your limits and respecting them. Because when you're drained, distracted, or chronically exhausted, you don't just suffer—your work does, your relationships do, your purpose does. Taking time for yourself is not selfish—it's strategic. It's maintenance. It's renewal. It's saying, I matter too, and backing that up with action.

When you invest in your well-being, you expand your capacity to be present, patient, and purposeful. You sharpen your focus, deepen your clarity, and strengthen your resilience. You lead better. You love better. You live better. So take the rest. Say no when you need to. Step into solitude when you're overwhelmed. Eat well. Sleep enough. Breathe deeply. Not because you're weak—but because you're wise. And because the people who depend on you don't just need your time—they need your wholeness.

SACRIFICE

Those who walk a lonely path grow weary of one's sacrifice.

Sacrifice can be noble, but it often comes with isolation. Giving deeply, especially without recognition, carries weight. When you sacrifice for others, the journey may feel lonely—but it is not in vain. Each quiet act of endurance builds strength, shapes character, and lights the way for those who follow. Not all sacrifices are celebrated. In fact, most aren't even seen. Those who walk a lonely path grow weary of one's sacrifice. To give of yourself consistently, to carry burdens for others, to show up when no one claps, is a quiet act of courage that is both beautiful and exhausting.

Sacrifice demands energy, time, and sometimes, your sense of self.

It asks you to put others first, to show up when you're tired, to offer more when you're already running on empty. And often, it offers little in return—at least, not in the ways you'd expect. There are no medals for holding families together, for staying strong when others fall apart, or for giving your best when the world isn't watching. But make no mistake: that kind of sacrifice is not wasted. It builds unseen legacies. It forms invisible bridges. It gives others a chance to walk where they never could have without you clearing the path first.

Yes, the path can feel lonely. But it is also sacred. You are shaping more than moments—you are shaping futures. Still, it's important to remember that noble sacrifice should not come at the cost of your soul. You must balance giving with grounding. You must allow space for your own needs, even as you serve others. Burnout doesn't equal loyalty. Silence doesn't equal strength. You are allowed to rest. You are allowed to ask for help. Because the strongest people are not those who sacrifice everything—but those who learn how to give without losing themselves in the process. And when your sacrifice feels unnoticed, remember: the seeds you plant in silence will bloom in someone else's tomorrow.

PEACE

In the depths of my silence, I am surrounded by the soothing melodies of sound.

Peace isn't the absence of noise—it's the ability to find harmony in stillness. Calm moments allow the world to fade and inner clarity to emerge. In silence, we hear the gentle rhythm of our thoughts, the subtle whisper of peace. It is in quiet that the soul finds its voice. Peace isn't found in the absence of sound—it's found in the absence of noise that doesn't belong to you.

In the depths of my silence, I am surrounded by the soothing melodies of sound. The world is loud—filled with obligations, notifications, expectations. But beyond that clamor is a quieter world, one that hums with the rhythm of your own being. A world you access only in stillness. We often equate silence with emptiness or discomfort. We avoid it, fill it, distract ourselves from it. But silence is not empty. It's full of everything you've been too busy to hear.

In silence, clarity is born.

It's where your true voice—beneath the roles, reactions, and routines—can rise. It's where answers arrive, not shouted, but softly. It's where the body exhales, the mind settles, and the heart speaks without filter. Peace is not something you stumble upon—it's something you create space for. It's choosing to pause when the world tells you to hurry. It's closing your eyes, not to sleep, but to see. It's stepping away, not to escape, but to return to yourself.

True peace doesn't require perfect conditions. It exists in the middle of chaos, in a single breath, in the still center of your soul. So don't fear the quiet. Go there often. Make it your sanctuary. Because in the depths of your silence, you'll hear something far more powerful than noise—you'll hear you.

ACTION

No journey is without obstacles, and no sacrifice is without reward, but none of that matters if you don't start moving.

The path to success will never be smooth, but motion is what gives it meaning. Action strips away excuses and gets to the core. Plans, dreams, and intentions are powerless without steps. Momentum creates opportunity. So, take the first stride, however small—it is the spark that ignites transformation. Every great journey begins the same way: with a step.

No journey is without obstacles, and no sacrifice is without reward, but none of that matters if you don't start moving. You can read every book, build the most elaborate vision board, gather all the right tools—and still remain exactly where you are if you refuse to take action. We live in a world addicted to preparation. We perfect the plan. We wait for the right timing. We gather feedback, second-guess ourselves, and wait some more. But planning without action is procrastination dressed in productivity's clothing.

Ideas don't change the world. Action does.

Movement matters—even if it's messy. Even if you don't know the outcome. Even if you trip the moment you begin. Because forward motion—any motion—breaks the grip of fear. It disrupts doubt. It fuels belief. The longer you wait, the heavier the weight of inaction becomes. And the longer you remain still, the harder it is to trust your ability to move.

Action doesn't promise perfection. It promises progress. You will encounter resistance. Obstacles are part of every worthwhile path. But once you're in motion, you begin to adapt. You respond. You grow stronger. You become the kind of person who builds as they go, who solves problems mid-stride, and who no longer waits for certainty before showing up.

And something else happens when you act: momentum builds. Small actions create movement. Movement creates energy. Energy invites opportunity. Before long, doors begin to open not because you knocked—but because you kept walking. Even your mindset changes. You stop asking, "What if I fail?" and begin asking, "What happens if I don't try?"

So start. Start afraid. Start unsure. Start underprepared. But start. Because all your potential, all your greatness, all your purpose—it only becomes real when you decide that standing still is no longer an option.

AWARENESS

Awareness is the mother of pain, love, and knowledge, so open your eyes and embrace the journey.

To be aware is to be alive. Awareness brings clarity, connection, and sometimes discomfort. Pain teaches, love binds, and knowledge frees—but none exist without the conscious act of noticing. Embrace awareness, for it is the gateway to growth, empathy, and wisdom. Awareness is both a gift and a challenge. It opens the door to beauty—but also to discomfort. It reveals joy, but also injustice. It illuminates truth, but also shadows we've been taught to ignore.

Awareness is the mother of pain, love, and knowledge. It births our deepest growth, because it forces us to see—really see—the world, others, and ourselves. To be aware is to be present. Not just in body, but in mind and heart. It's choosing to pay attention when it's easier to look away. It's noticing not just what's happening, but why it's happening. It's listening without preparing your defense. It's witnessing without turning away.

Awareness invites accountability. You cannot change what you will not acknowledge.

You cannot heal what you won't confront. But when you're awake—when your eyes, ears, and heart are open—you position yourself for transformation. This journey isn't always easy. Awareness brings pain, yes. But it also births wisdom. It fuels empathy. It deepens connection. And over time, it becomes the compass that helps you walk through the world with integrity, intention, and compassion.

So don't fear awareness. Step into it. Because the most powerful breakthroughs always begin with the words, "I see it now."

CONFIDENCE

To believe in oneself is the strongest weapon against failure.

Confidence doesn't guarantee success, but without it, success is almost impossible. Belief in oneself is a shield against doubt and a spark for bold action. Confidence isn't arrogance—it's trust in your value and potential. When the world questions you, let your self-belief answer. The loudest critic is often inside your own head.

To believe in oneself is the strongest weapon against failure. Because when self-doubt rises, when obstacles push back, when the world questions your worth—confidence is the anchor that keeps you grounded and the engine that keeps you moving. Confidence isn't about thinking you're better than others—it's about knowing you're worthy of trying, growing, and showing up fully. It's not the absence of fear, but the presence of belief.

Without confidence, even the most gifted individuals stay silent. They pass on opportunity. They shrink their presence. But with confidence, even the imperfect can thrive—because they dare to begin.

Confidence is built, not born.

It's earned through small acts of courage, through choosing yourself before others do, through showing up even when you're uncertain. It's trusting your instincts, your experiences, your voice. You will stumble. You will question. But confidence reminds you that your worth is not based on a flawless performance—it's rooted in the unwavering truth that you are enough, even in progress.

Let your confidence be quiet, not boastful. Let it speak through consistency. Through resilience. Through authenticity. And when the voices of doubt grow loud, let your belief in yourself grow louder. Because no one can do what you're here to do—not like you. Not with your heart. Not with your voice. Own it.

BEAUTY

I see colors, I see beauty; I most certainly see someone as beautiful as you.

B eauty is both seen and felt. It's a recognition of presence, individuality, and radiance. When we truly see someone—beyond the surface—we connect to something timeless. Let these words be a mirror to your worth: you are seen, and you are beautiful.

Beauty isn't defined by symmetry, style, or trend. It's not reserved for magazine covers, filtered photos, or curated appearances. Real beauty—the kind that moves you, the kind that makes people stop and take notice—lives in presence, energy, and truth. I see colors, I see beauty; I most certainly see someone as beautiful as you. These words are more than a compliment—they are a reminder. That beauty is not only something you have—it's something you are.

It's in the way your eyes light up when you talk about something you love. In the laugh that erupts before you can stop it. In the way you show up—authentic, flawed, honest. It's in your scars, your stretch marks, your soft heart, and your sharp mind. Beauty lives in your resilience. In the kindness you offer when you're tired. In the space you hold for others, and the strength it takes to hold space for yourself.

Yet too often, we forget this. We look in mirrors and measure ourselves by impossible standards. We diminish our beauty by comparing it to someone else's highlight reel. We let someone else's definition of "enough" dim our own light. But beauty is not comparison—it is presence. It's not perfection—it's essence.

When you recognize beauty in someone, it's often because it reflects something already inside you.

The ability to see beauty in others comes from the practice of honoring it in yourself. So look again—not at your flaws, but at your fullness. See yourself not as society has labeled you, but as you truly are: radiant, worthy, and already beautiful. Let that be your standard. And when you meet others, look deeper than the surface. Speak beauty into them. Remind them. Because sometimes, a single truth said aloud—"You are beautiful"—can change the way someone walks through the world.

COMMITMENT

Pour out everything, including your heart and soul, and walk away knowing you left no stone unturned.

True commitment is not measured by outcomes but by effort. Give fully—to love, create, serve, and fight with everything you have. And when the moment ends, peace comes not from success or failure, but from knowing you held nothing back. That is the freedom of wholehearted living. Half-hearted effort will never deliver full-hearted results.

Pour out everything, including your heart and soul, and walk away knowing you left no stone unturned. That's not just commitment—that's liberation. Because nothing haunts the spirit more than the question, "What if I'd tried a little harder?" Commitment is not just about showing up. It's about pouring yourself in, fully, even when it's uncomfortable, uncertain, or unrewarded. It's saying, "I will give this my all, not because I am guaranteed success, but because it is worth it."

In love, it means vulnerability. In your work, it means intention. In your passion, it means consistency. And in your values, it means conviction. When you live with that kind of devotion, something shifts. The pressure of perfection falls away. Because the goal isn't to guarantee a win—it's to guarantee your integrity. You walk away not wondering what could have been, but standing in the truth of what was. You gave. You tried. You risked. You stayed.

True commitment is not easy. It will stretch you. It will disappoint you.

But it will also transform you. It builds strength where fear once lived. It clarifies purpose. It eliminates regret. It deepens your sense of self and strengthens your sense of what matters. And when the dust settles, whether the result is triumph or heartbreak, you'll be able to look in the mirror and say with certainty: "I gave it everything. I am proud. I am free." Because to live fully committed is to live without holding back. And that kind of living leaves nothing wasted.

INTIMACY

I walk to avoid standing; I speak to avoid silence, but I love for the sake of being closer to you.

Intimacy explores the layers of human connection. We move, we speak, but love is what draws us near. It's not just about presence—it's about vulnerability and the desire to be seen, heard, and held. In love, we find the courage to stop running and simply be—with someone who sees our soul. We move through life in motion—running from vulnerability, speaking to avoid silence, performing to mask what's unspoken. But love asks something different of us. It asks us to stay.

I walk to avoid standing; I speak to avoid silence, but I love for the sake of being closer to you. This is the paradox of intimacy: the closer we want to be, the more tempted we are to shield ourselves. We move to escape stillness, we talk to fill space, but deep down, we're longing for someone who sees through all of it and chooses us anyway. Intimacy is not just physical—it's emotional. It's spiritual. It's psychological safety in human form. It is found in quiet moments of honesty. In glances that don't demand words. In the courage to sit with someone else's truth without needing to fix it.

True intimacy isn't about knowing the facts of someone's life—it's about knowing how they feel their life.

It's the difference between hearing and listening, touching and holding, seeing and witnessing. It requires stillness. Vulnerability. A willingness to stop performing and start revealing. And when we find that kind of connection—the kind where we are safe enough to stop running, to fall silent, to simply be—we discover love not as a feeling, but as a sanctuary.

So stay a little longer. Listen a little deeper. Let someone all the way in. Because the greatest closeness isn't built through constant motion—it's found in the moments when you choose not to walk or speak, but simply exist... together.

HAPPINESS

If happiness is overrated, count me in as another over-achiever.

J oy should never be minimized or dismissed. This flips cynicism on its head, celebrating happiness as a worthy pursuit. If loving life, finding peace, and feeling fulfilled makes one an "overachiever," then so be it. Chase joy unapologetically. Happiness isn't overrated—it's a sign that you're living fully and on your own terms.

In a world that glorifies hustle and rewards burnout, happiness is often treated like an afterthought. It's framed as a luxury—something you earn once you've "made it," once you've achieved enough, sacrificed enough, proved enough. But what if happiness wasn't a finish line?

If happiness is overrated, count me in as another overachiever. Because in truth, happiness is not a distraction from meaning—it is meaning. It is not an escape from responsibility—it's what gives responsibility purpose. And it is not reserved for the lucky—it's created, chosen, and cultivated by those who believe they are worthy of experiencing joy now, not later.

Happiness isn't a constant high. It's not a glittering, picture-perfect life. It's presence. It's alignment.

It's the quiet contentment of knowing you're living in a way that feels true to you. And while the world may try to sell you happiness in packages, promotions, or praise, real happiness isn't purchased—it's practiced. It's found in early morning light. In laughter that catches you off guard. In the way your chest softens when you're with someone who sees you. In giving without needing to receive. In choosing rest without guilt. In choosing yourself without apology.

To pursue happiness boldly in this world is an act of resistance. Cynicism has become a social currency, and suffering a badge of honor. But you were not born to be exhausted, depleted, or endlessly striving for a life that doesn't make you feel alive. You were born to feel the full range of joy. To savor the sweetness of simple moments. To experience pleasure without permission. To know that fulfillment isn't selfish—it's foundational.

Your happiness doesn't need to be loud. It doesn't need to be explained. It only needs to be yours. So laugh without restraint. Breathe without apology. Find the people, places, and practices that return you to yourself—and protect them fiercely. Because if joy is a rebellion in a weary world, let yours be unstoppable.

VIGILANCE

Guard your thoughts; it's the bridge between nightmares and dreams.

Your mind is the gatekeeper of your reality. What you allow in shapes who you become. Thoughts can either lead us to fear or to vision. Be intentional with your focus—discipline your thinking and you'll build a path toward the life you imagine. Let vigilance over your mind protect your purpose. You are what you think—more than most people realize.

Guard your thoughts; it's the bridge between nightmares and dreams. Every reality you build starts in the mind. Every fear, every breakthrough, every quiet victory or loud defeat—it all begins with a single thought, repeated over time. The mind is both soil and seed. What you plant, grows. What you nourish, blooms. What you allow to take root—be it doubt or hope, despair or vision—eventually shapes the world you live in, whether you're aware of it or not.

That's why vigilance is more than awareness—it's protection. It's intentional curation of what enters your mental space. In a world flooded with opinions, images, comparisons, and noise, the most radical thing you can do is protect your inner world with discipline.

Vigilance doesn't mean living in fear. It means living with clarity.

It's knowing when to switch off the voice of negativity and tune in to a higher frequency—the one aligned with your values, your vision, and your truth. When your thoughts go unguarded, you risk giving power to the wrong narratives. You let old fears play like familiar songs. You rehearse limitations until they become identity. But when you begin to think deliberately—when you learn to stop the spiral before it picks up speed—you start creating space. Space for peace. For hope. For new dreams. For grounded action.

So guard your thoughts like you would your future—because they are the same. What you think consistently becomes what you believe. And what you believe becomes what you build. Be vigilant.

SUPPORT

It's never a good idea to suffer in silence; seek assistance from trusted partners.

S trength doesn't mean doing everything alone. Openness, connection, and vulnerability are signs of wisdom, not weakness. When challenges come, reaching out provides perspective, strength, and relief. Together, we're more capable, more resilient, and never truly alone. Pain is loudest when held in silence. It's never a good idea to suffer in silence; seek assistance from trusted partners. That sentence is not just advice—it's a lifeline. In a world that often romanticizes self-sufficiency, we forget that solitude, when unspoken and unshared, can quietly evolve into suffering.

We convince ourselves we'll figure it out. That we don't want to burden anyone. That others are too busy, or wouldn't understand. And so, we keep quiet. We endure in silence. And we slowly begin to believe that silence is strength. But it's not.

Real strength is knowing when to open your mouth and say, "I'm not okay." It's recognizing that asking for help is not surrender—it's strategy. It's choosing support not because you're falling apart, but because you're wise enough to know that none of us can carry everything alone.

Support doesn't mean you're weak—it means you're connected.

It means you've built relationships based on trust. It means you've created a safety net for the moments when life hits harder than expected. And sometimes, support doesn't look like advice or answers. It looks like someone sitting quietly beside you, someone who reminds you through their presence that you're not alone. It's someone checking in, someone remembering your story, someone reminding you of your strength when yours feels out of reach.

The most powerful people are not the ones who never fall—they're the ones who know who to call when they do. So build your circle. Choose wisely, but don't wait for perfection. Find the people who hold space without judgment, who listen more than they speak, who aren't afraid of your mess or your silence. And be that person for others, too.

We were not designed to walk life's path in isolation. We are communal by nature, wired for belonging, strengthened by support. No matter how capable you are, your soul still needs a place to rest, a voice to hear you, and hands that hold you up. Don't let pride or fear keep you in isolation. Speak up. Reach out. Because healing happens faster when you stop trying to do it all alone.

GROWTH

Focus your mind and thoughts and watch your enterprise grow.

E very great outcome begins with intention. Mental clarity and directed energy are the foundations of progress. Whether you're building a business, a relationship, or yourself, your focus determines your future. Where attention flows, growth follows—so focus with purpose and watch success take root. Growth doesn't happen by accident. It responds to intention, thrives on discipline, and multiplies through clarity.

Focus your mind and thoughts and watch your enterprise grow. Whether that enterprise is your career, your creative work, your family, your character—or your healing—it all starts in the same place: the mind. A scattered focus will scatter your progress. But a focused mind is a force that multiplies every ounce of effort into results.

It's easy to be busy without moving forward. You can chase a hundred distractions and confuse motion with momentum. But real growth—measurable, lasting, soul-level growth—demands direction. It requires that you pause, align, and pour your energy with purpose. That starts with your thoughts. Your inner dialogue becomes your blueprint. If your thoughts are chaotic, unclear, self-doubting, your actions will follow. But when your thoughts are sharp, centered, and committed, your actions begin to build something solid.

Every major success begins in the mind of someone who dared to believe it was possible.

Before the business took shape, the relationship deepened, or the transformation happened—someone decided to focus. Not half-heartedly. Not casually. But with daily, deliberate attention. Growth is not always fast. But it is always faithful to the focused. What you water, grows. What you give energy to, becomes stronger. What you think about consistently becomes the lens through which you shape your world. So choose your focus like your future depends on it—because it does.

REGRETLESS

Live without regrets and enjoy the one-way trip we call life.

Life moves forward—there are no rewinds or do-overs. Embrace each moment, make bold choices, and release guilt tied to the past. Regret weighs down the journey, while acceptance lightens the load. Live fully, love freely, and trust that every step—right or wrong—adds depth to your story. Regret is a quiet thief. It doesn't storm in and steal your joy—it whispers, slowly, consistently, telling you that your past disqualifies your present.

Live without regrets and enjoy the one-way trip we call life. This journey has no reverse gear. There are no second takes. No reset buttons. Only now—and whatever you choose to make of it. Living without regret doesn't mean living without mistakes. You will misstep. You will say the wrong thing, trust the wrong person, turn down the right path too late. But those moments aren't the end of your story. They are your story.

Regretless living is about owning the past, not erasing it.

It's about choosing to learn instead of linger. It's forgiving yourself for not knowing better when you didn't—and giving yourself the grace to do better now that you do. It's waking up each day and saying, "Today is still mine. My power is not in perfection—it's in presence." Too many people spend their energy rewriting the past in their minds instead of writing the future with their actions. But the past doesn't need edits. It needs understanding. You were doing your best. And even when you weren't, you were human.

So make bold choices. Speak the truth. Take the risk. Say yes to what excites you and no to what drains you. Apologize when needed. Let go when it's time. And above all, keep moving forward. This is a one-way trip. Don't spend it apologizing for the miles behind you. Use them to fuel the miles ahead.

Optimism

If history has taught us anything, the future is ripe for progress.

The past is filled with lessons of resilience, growth, and change. Even in dark chapters, humanity has found ways to rise. Optimism is not naivety—it's an informed belief that better is possible. Let history inspire you to believe in the potential of tomorrow. Hope isn't fragile—it's forged.

If history has taught us anything, the future is ripe for progress. We don't have to guess whether change is possible—we have proof. Over and over again, humanity has stood in the rubble of conflict, crisis, and collapse and chosen to rebuild. Again and again, we've faced impossible odds and made it through. That's what optimism is. It's not blind faith. It's not toxic positivity. It's the stubborn, steady belief that progress is not only possible—it's earned. That tomorrow can be better because we've made it better before.

Look at the pages of history. You'll find injustice—but also the courage that rose to confront it. You'll find failure—but also resilience that refused to quit.

For every mistake, there's a correction. For every wound, a healer. For every fall, a comeback.

Optimism doesn't ask you to ignore reality. It asks you to recognize that reality is not finished. That where you are is not where you have to stay. That no matter how dark the night has been, morning still returns. It's a mindset, not a mood. And it's one of the most powerful tools you can carry. Because what you expect affects what you attempt. What you believe influences what you build. If you believe change is possible, you become the kind of person who creates it.

So when the noise gets loud and the world feels heavy, remember: your optimism is not foolish—it's foundational. It's your refusal to accept that the story is over. It's your commitment to write the next chapter—brighter, bolder, better.

INSPIRATION

Surround yourself with successful thinkers and enrich your mind with the power of inspiration.

Your environment shapes your mindset. Seek out minds that challenge, uplift, and inspire. When you engage with those who dream boldly and act wisely, their energy becomes contagious. Feed your mind with powerful thoughts, and watch your own aspirations take flight. You become what you're exposed to. Your thoughts, your ideas, your ambitions—they're shaped by the people you allow closest to your inner world.

Surround yourself with successful thinkers and enrich your mind with the power of inspiration. The energy, creativity, and belief systems of others can either dull your vision or elevate your potential. Choose wisely. Inspiration is a fuel. It doesn't replace work, but it makes the work feel worth it. It stirs something in you that reminds you of what's possible. And the people who carry that spark—the thinkers, the builders, the dreamers—help light the fire in you.

But inspiration isn't passive. You don't just wait for it—you create the conditions for it to grow. That means curating your circle. Reading what challenges you. Listening to conversations that stretch you. Learning from those who've failed and tried again. Staying close to people who speak life into your potential and mirror your courage back to you.

Great minds don't just think alike—they ignite one another.

And the more you immerse yourself in inspired environments, the more your mindset shifts from limitation to innovation, from fear to faith, from waiting to doing. You don't need to do it all alone. Inspiration is meant to be shared, multiplied, passed on. And when you become someone who feeds on it, you also become someone who feeds others with it. So find those people. Be that person. Stay in that energy. Because what enters your mind, shapes your life.

DIVERSITY

The danger of monolithic thoughts is the absence of competing ideas.

U niformity may seem comfortable, but it stifles innovation. Diversity of thought is essential for growth, creativity, and progress. When all perspectives are identical, we lose the richness of debate and the breakthroughs born from challenge. Seek out different voices—they sharpen wisdom. Sameness is easy—but progress has never been born from ease.

The danger of monolithic thoughts is the absence of competing ideas. When everyone at the table sees the world through the same lens, speaks the same language, and validates the same assumptions, we don't grow—we echo. And in the echo chamber, creativity withers. Possibility shrinks. Wisdom stays dormant.

True diversity goes beyond demographics. It's not just about who is in the room—it's about what is heard in the room. It's about making space for different backgrounds, values, approaches, and ways of thinking. It's knowing that challenge is not conflict—it's an invitation to expand.

Diversity of thought is where solutions are refined, empathy is built, and innovation is sparked.

When different ideas meet, they sharpen each other. Friction isn't the enemy—friction is the fire that forges breakthroughs. But this kind of diversity requires humility. It asks us to listen longer, speak slower, and resist the urge to defend what's familiar. It challenges us to examine our blind spots and to ask, What perspective am I missing? rather than How do I convince them I'm right?

When you surround yourself only with those who agree, you create a reality that feels safe but is fundamentally incomplete. And in that safety, complacency grows. So make it your practice to invite new ideas, even when they feel uncomfortable. Make it your posture to listen to those who challenge you with respect. And make it your mission to never let comfort be the reason you stop evolving. Because diversity is not a threat to unity—it's the foundation of it.

OPENNESS

The fear of change is the architect of failure; be open to ideas as a catalyst for change.

C hange is not the enemy—resistance to it is. Openness is a mindset for evolution. New ideas are the seeds of progress, and openness allows them to grow. Let curiosity replace fear, and you'll discover that change isn't a threat—it's an opportunity in disguise. The world doesn't stand still, and neither should you.

The fear of change is the architect of failure; be open to ideas as a catalyst for change. Growth demands movement. Evolution requires flexibility. And at the core of every transformation—personal or societal—is a willingness to be open.

Openness doesn't mean abandoning your principles. It means examining them.

It means welcoming new information, trying unfamiliar methods, and saying, "Maybe there's a better way." Fear often masquerades as logic when we're confronted with change. We convince ourselves that staying the same is safer, smarter, more efficient. But progress has never come from the familiar. Every innovation, every step forward, every new chapter has begun with someone brave enough to be open.

Openness is the soil in which ideas take root. It allows creativity to stretch, relationships to deepen, and perspective to shift. It doesn't mean you say yes to everything—but it does mean you resist the urge to say no just because something feels different. When you lead with curiosity instead of control, you make space for breakthroughs. When you lean into the unknown rather than retreating, you step into the future with intention instead of fear.

So ask more questions. Consider more voices. Loosen your grip on what you think must stay the same, and allow room for what might be better. Because when you choose openness, you choose possibility.

STRENGTH

Some of the strongest voices in the face of adversity can often result in silence.

S trength isn't always loud—it's often quiet, steady, and unseen. Courageous individuals carry weight when standing against overwhelming odds. Sometimes, even the bravest fall silent—not from defeat, but from exhaustion or reflection. Let us not mistake silence for weakness, but recognize it as a pause in the presence of enduring strength. Strength doesn't always roar. Sometimes, it sits in silence, breathing through the weight of the moment, gathering itself before speaking again.

Some of the strongest voices in the face of adversity can often result in silence. Not because they've lost the will—but because they've carried too much, for too long, and they need a moment to simply be. We often expect the strongest people to always be resilient, always articulate, always present. But true strength isn't constant output—it's honest pause. It's knowing when to speak and when to retreat, when to push and when to protect your energy.

Those who carry others, who advocate, lead, and sacrifice, often do so without recognition.

They give without asking. They speak up until their voices tremble. And when they fall silent, it's not a sign that they're weak—it's a signal that they've earned a breath. Silence, in this context, is not surrender. It is space. It is recalibration. It's the sacred pause where the strongest among us gather their thoughts and ready themselves to rise again.

So when you see someone fall quiet, don't assume they've given up. Respect their stillness. Hold space for their strength to rebuild. Because strength isn't always visible—and it's never just about what's shown. It's about what's endured, what's held together, and what keeps showing up, even if it can't speak today. And if that quiet person is you, let this be your reminder: Your strength is not diminished by your stillness. It may, in fact, be defined by it.

TRANQUILITY

The power of silence breathes insanity into some while giving others the gift of therapy.

Silence is a double-edged sword. For some, it is discomforting and chaotic; for others, it is healing and restorative. Tranquility invites us to be still, to listen, and to reconnect with ourselves. Whether it soothes or unsettles depends on what we bring into it. But within that silence lies the potential for peace. Silence is not empty—it is layered, complex, and deeply personal.

The power of silence breathes insanity into some while giving others the gift of therapy. It is one of life's most paradoxical forces. To some, silence feels like loneliness. To others, it's liberation. To some, it echoes with everything they've avoided. To others, it hums with healing.

Tranquility is not the absence of sound—it's the presence of stillness.

It's a space where you are no longer reacting, no longer running, no longer performing. It's the pause where thoughts rise to the surface and emotions get the room they need to breathe. But silence isn't always peaceful at first. When the noise stops, everything you've been avoiding tends to speak louder. That's why many resist silence—it forces us to face ourselves. It exposes our inner dialogue, our buried questions, our unmet needs. Yet, when we learn to sit with it—not judge it, not flee from it—it begins to soften. It begins to soothe.

The beauty of tranquility is not that it erases chaos, but that it offers a counterweight to it. It teaches you that you don't always have to respond. That healing doesn't always happen in conversation—it sometimes happens in breath. That you don't have to solve everything today—you just have to be here. So when silence comes, welcome it like a mirror. Let it show you what's within. Let it hold what you can't name. Let it be the space where you remember yourself again. Because in the calm, in the quiet, in the gentle return to stillness—peace finds its voice.

BALANCE

Where there is darkness, there is light; where there is chaos, there is hope; where there is hatred, there is love; any questions?

Life is a dance of dualities. Opposing forces are not just inevitable—they are necessary. Darkness highlights the power of light, and pain teaches the value of joy. When we understand this balance, we stop resisting life's contrasts and start learning from them. There's always another side—look for it. Life doesn't unfold in straight lines or perfect symmetry—it moves in contrast. And within that contrast lies its greatest beauty, and its deepest lessons.

Where there is darkness, there is light; where there is chaos, there is hope; where there is hatred, there is love; any questions? This isn't just a poetic truth—it's a roadmap for understanding the full experience of being alive. We're taught to fear discomfort. To flee from pain. To eliminate what doesn't feel good. But balance isn't about avoidance—it's about awareness. It's about understanding that joy and sorrow are not enemies, but companions. That peace doesn't mean the absence of struggle—it means the presence of grace in the middle of it.

Every high is meaningful because you've known the low. Every calm is sweeter because you've weathered the storm. Every act of love becomes more profound when you've seen the face of hate and chosen to love anyway.

> **Balance is the ability to hold both. To stand in tension without breaking. To look at the full spectrum of life and say, "I choose to learn from all of it."**

It doesn't mean neutrality—it means wisdom. It means knowing that while you can't always control what happens, you can choose how to respond. And often, that response comes from seeing the other side of the moment you're in. If you're in the dark—look for the light. If you're overwhelmed—trust that hope still lives somewhere beneath the noise. If you're angry—remember that love has not left the world, even if it's quieter today.

Balance reminds us that nothing is one-dimensional. That every hardship carries a lesson, every ending makes room for a beginning, and every trial has the potential to shape something resilient, beautiful, and whole. So the next time life feels lopsided, remember: the opposite exists. It always has. Sometimes, you just have to shift your gaze to see it.

HONESTY

The only way to express the truth is with the truth.

There is no substitute for authenticity. Truth cannot be dressed up, diluted, or manipulated. To live honestly is to speak with integrity and act with transparency. The truth may not always be easy, but it is always powerful—and it always finds its way. Truth doesn't need decoration. It doesn't need to be softened or rebranded to be real. In fact, the more it's diluted, the more it loses its power. The only way to express the truth is with the truth. Not half of it. Not the convenient version. Not what's easier to say or what sounds better to the room. Just truth—raw, unfiltered, and free of disguise.

Honesty is not about being blunt. It's about being real. It's about showing up with integrity, even when it's uncomfortable. It's about having the courage to say what's hard because you value clarity over comfort, and principle over performance. In a world full of posturing and pretense, honesty stands out—not because it's loud, but because it's rare. It doesn't demand trust—it earns it. It doesn't manipulate—it liberates. And most of all, it doesn't bend under pressure.

When you speak with honesty, you speak with alignment.

Your words match your values. Your actions match your intent. And while it may cost you temporary approval, it buys you long-term peace. Living honestly doesn't mean you always get it right. It means you're willing to admit when you don't. It means you own your truth before anyone else can try to twist it. It means your reputation isn't built on image—it's built on substance. And the beautiful thing about truth is this: it doesn't need to be defended. It only needs to be lived.

So choose honesty. Speak it. Walk in it. Let it be your baseline. Because the truth doesn't always make life easier—but it always makes it real.

FLEXIBILITY

There is no such thing as a final solution. They are all efforts towards a better outcome.

L ife is a process, not a destination. Every solution is just a step-pingstone toward progress—not perfection. Flexibility allows us to adapt, improve, and refine our paths without becoming paralyzed by the need for finality. Embrace iteration, and you'll discover that progress is built on continuous evolution. We are conditioned to seek resolution—the neat ending, the perfect answer, the moment when everything finally makes sense and stays that way. But life doesn't work like that.

There is no such thing as a final solution. They are all efforts toward a better outcome. Every fix is temporary. Every decision opens new doors. Every solution leads to new complexity. The goal isn't to arrive at certainty—it's to move with purpose, knowing full well that certainty is often an illusion.

Flexibility is not just a skill—it's a survival strategy.

It is the ability to shift without crumbling. To revise without shame. To adapt without abandoning your core. Rigid thinking may offer comfort, but it leads to fragility. It says, "This is the only way." Flexibility says, "There might be a better way tomorrow, and that's okay." Being flexible doesn't mean lacking conviction. It means being mature enough to refine your convictions when growth demands it. It means holding onto your values while adjusting your approach. It's knowing the difference between being committed and being stuck.

The most successful people—leaders, creators, visionaries—aren't the ones who had all the answers at the start. They're the ones who listened when the path told them to turn. They're the ones who shifted their strategy, recalibrated their plans, and tried again with new perspective. And because of that, they stayed in motion while others stalled. Flexibility invites learning. It gives you permission to evolve. It says that missteps aren't failures—they're feedback. That changing direction isn't a sign of confusion—it's a sign of responsiveness.

When you release the pressure to get it exactly right the first time, you free yourself to grow into the version of yourself who can get it right with time. And that's where real progress lives—not in fixed destinations, but in your willingness to keep stepping forward, adjusting the path, and staying open to what's next. So trade your obsession with finality for a commitment to refinement. Stay open. Stay curious. Stay in motion. Because every time you adjust, you're not abandoning your goal—you're getting closer to it.

INGENUITY

When life gives you marbles instead of crystals, avoid being uninspired. Roll them down the road and follow them to a better future.

Ingenuity thrives in unexpected moments. Limitations can become opportunities when we reimagine them creatively. What you're given may not be perfect, but it can lead to something greater if you stay innovative. Use what you have. Innovate, pivot, and let inspiration guide you where perfection never could. We don't always get what we wanted. But sometimes, what we're given holds a gift we didn't know we needed.

When life gives you marbles instead of crystals, avoid being uninspired. Roll them down the road and follow them to a better future. The message is clear: don't miss the opportunity just because it came wrapped in the unexpected. Ingenuity isn't about having the best materials. It's about making something meaningful with whatever is in your hands. It's the child who builds a spaceship from cardboard.

The entrepreneur who turns a garage into a global brand. The survivor who crafts strength out of struggle.

When we get caught up waiting for the perfect moment, the perfect tools, or the perfect conditions, we end up paralyzed.

Ingenuity moves anyway. It uses what's available. It pivots. It plays. It doesn't ask, "Why don't I have more?" It asks, "What can I do with what I've got?" Innovation is born not from abundance, but from constraint. It emerges in the gap between challenge and curiosity. When you allow yourself to experiment, to try, to risk doing it differently, you often discover something far more powerful than a perfect plan—you discover possibility.

Let go of the idea that you need crystal clarity before you begin. Start with marbles. Start with mess. Start with less-than-ideal. Then roll them forward and follow their momentum. Because what begins as limitation often becomes liberation in the hands of someone creative enough to believe in a better future.

EMPATHY

I walked a mile in your shoes, and what did I learn? That walking in someone else's footsteps is not my own.

Empathy is about understanding—not imitation. Even when we try to experience another's life, we still bring our own perspective. True empathy honors differences rather than assuming sameness. It's not about becoming someone else; it's about respecting their journey while staying grounded in your own. Empathy is not pretending to be someone else—it's honoring who they are while standing fully in who you are.

I walked a mile in your shoes, and what did I learn? That walking in someone else's footsteps is not my own. True empathy isn't about borrowing someone's pain or trying to fully inhabit their story. It's about witnessing their journey with reverence and care—without losing yourself in the process.

When we confuse empathy with imitation, we reduce someone's experience to our own frame of reference.

No matter how deeply we listen or how closely we relate, we will never carry their exact weight. And that's not a weakness—it's reality. Empathy doesn't require full understanding—it requires presence. It's the willingness to say, "I may not fully grasp what you're feeling, but I'll stand beside you as you feel it." It's not about fixing. It's not about comparing. It's not about saying, "I know how you feel." It's about saying, "I see you. I hear you. I honor what this means to you."

Empathy also creates boundaries. It allows us to remain connected without becoming consumed. It teaches us to carry compassion without collapsing under someone else's pain. And when we offer that to others, we create the space for healing—not by changing their story, but by allowing them to tell it in their own words, in their own time. So don't try to be someone else in the name of empathy. Be yourself—present, open, compassionate—and let that be enough. Because real empathy doesn't erase the distance between us. It builds a bridge across it.

CAUTION

Don't be fooled by the light in the tunnel when common sense and logic keep pulling you back from the jaws of disaster.

Hope can sometimes blur judgment. We must weigh optimism against reason. Not every light leads to salvation—some lead to traps. When your instincts and logic raise red flags, listen. Caution is not fear—it's wisdom, sharpened by experience, protecting you from avoidable harm. Not every light at the end of the tunnel leads to safety. Sometimes, it's the glow of something you should be walking away from.

Don't be fooled by the light in the tunnel when common sense and logic keep pulling you back from the jaws of disaster. It's easy to confuse desire for direction. When we want something badly enough, even danger can start to look like a doorway. That's why caution matters. It's not a lack of faith—it's the application of wisdom. It's the ability to hold hope in one hand and reason in the other. Because while faith propels you forward, logic protects your path.

Caution asks you to listen to the quiet internal voice that says, "Something isn't right."

The one that notices the red flags others call ambition. The one that doesn't get swept up in enthusiasm but pauses to ask the hard questions: Is this wise? Is this safe? Is this real? To live cautiously doesn't mean living small. It means living smart. It means trusting your instincts, honoring your life experience, and making choices not from desperation or denial—but from discernment.

Sometimes the brave thing isn't charging forward. It's stopping. It's waiting. It's walking away before you lose something you can't get back. So don't confuse hesitation with weakness. Don't dismiss caution as cowardice. Because sometimes, the strongest thing you can do is say no to what you once thought you couldn't live without.

INNER STRENGTH

In the hour of darkness, the only light you need is the one from within.

When the world goes dim and guidance feels distant, your inner strength becomes your compass. The most dependable source of resilience is already within. In moments of fear or confusion, look inward. Trust your values, your courage, and your intuition—they are the light that never fades. The world can grow quiet when you need answers most. Doors close. People disappear. Certainty vanishes.

In the hour of darkness, the only light you need is the one from within. When everything around you feels unstable, when nothing makes sense, and when no one can tell you what to do next—that's when your inner strength steps in. It's not flashy. It's not loud. It doesn't arrive with applause or affirmation. It shows up in quiet conviction. In the decision to keep going, even when no one's watching. In the whispered reminder to yourself: I've made it through worse.

Inner strength isn't about always knowing what to do—it's about knowing you will figure it out.

It's the trust you've built through every past storm. The voice that says, "You've been here before. You know how to stand up again." Those who nurture inner strength find that external darkness or difficulty no longer feels insurmountable. The internal light—their steadfast optimism, deeply-held values, and unwavering self-respect—becomes an unyielding beacon. By cultivating this inner resilience, we become capable of navigating even the darkest nights, confident that the source of strength and guidance needed lies within.

This kind of strength can't be borrowed or bought. It's earned—through endurance, through heartbreak, through choosing to rise when staying down would be easier. And while the world may not see your inner fight, you know it. You feel it. And eventually, that internal flame becomes bright enough to light the path forward—not just for yourself, but for others, too. So when the lights go out and everything external fades, lean inward. That light is yours. That strength is real. And that voice—the one that refuses to quit—isn't just hope.

BOLDNESS

Why wait for permission when forgiveness is easier to gain; charge headfirst into the darkness and let faith guide your way.

Boldness thrives in the space between risk and conviction. It dares you to act, even when the path is unclear. Waiting for approval can cost you opportunity. Faith—whether in yourself, your mission, or something greater—can light the way when logic falls short. Be bold, move forward, and deal with consequences as they come. Boldness begins where hesitation ends.

Why wait for permission when forgiveness is easier to gain? It's not a statement of rebellion—it's a declaration of agency. Because the truth is, many of life's most meaningful moments don't come after a green light—they come after you decide to go anyway. Boldness is not arrogance. It's not recklessness. It's clarity, wrapped in courage, willing to move even when conditions aren't ideal and outcomes aren't guaranteed. It's the decision to trust your voice, your purpose, your timing—even when no one else sees it yet.

You don't need a title to lead. You don't need validation to speak. You don't need certainty to begin.

Boldness is often lonely at first. It puts you ahead of approval. It asks you to risk being misunderstood. To walk into spaces not yet ready for you. To believe in your mission more than your comfort. But boldness doesn't apologize for moving—it invites others to rise with you. There will be resistance. You'll be told to slow down, to wait, to be "realistic." But boldness isn't about being reckless—it's about being relentless. It's about letting faith lead where logic ends. Faith in yourself. Faith in the idea. Faith in the belief that impact often begins in the shadows, long before the spotlight arrives. And yes, sometimes you will make mistakes.

But boldness isn't afraid of failure—it makes peace with it. Because failure means you tried. You showed up. You took the step while others stood still. So stop waiting. Stop shrinking your brilliance to make others comfortable. Stop holding your ideas hostage while you wait for permission to be great. The world doesn't need more people waiting. It needs more people willing. Willing to lead. Willing to speak. Willing to dare. Willing to go first. Because boldness doesn't ask if the world is ready. It simply moves—and lets the world catch up.

HOPE

In the valley of the wicked, I stand undisturbed by the fray, with a renewed hope that righteousness will save the day.

Hope is defiance in the face of despair. It paints a picture of unwavering faith even in hostile surroundings. Righteousness may feel distant, but standing firm in your values is a declaration that good still matters. Hope doesn't ignore evil—it resists it. And in resistance, it draws strength. Hope is not a whisper. It is a war cry.

In the valley of the wicked, I stand undisturbed by the fray. That is not denial. That is discipline. Hope in this context is not passive—it is an act of resistance. It is choosing to believe in goodness when all signs suggest giving up. In a world so often shaped by cynicism, hope is revolutionary. It dares to say, "This isn't the end." It stands tall in dark places and insists that light still has a role to play.

Hope doesn't erase struggle—it carries you through it.

Hope is the force that keeps you grounded when justice is delayed. It's what steadies your voice when truth feels buried. It's what keeps your soul intact when systems are broken, when people disappoint you, when change seems slow and suffering seems endless. Righteousness doesn't always win quickly. But hope doesn't need fast—it needs faith. And when that faith lives in your bones, you can walk through chaos with your peace intact. You can stand surrounded by doubt and still speak conviction. You can look at a failing world and believe not only that healing is possible—but that it's already underway.

Because hope isn't foolish. It's forward-facing. It's rooted in the belief that what is good will prevail—not because it's easy, but because people like you continue to believe, continue to stand, continue to act. So if you find yourself in the valley—stay standing. Hope isn't blind. It's brave.

VISION

If tomorrow was yesterday and yesterday was today, then the future is written, and history has already spoken.

This reflection plays with time to reveal a deeper truth: vision is rooted in awareness. Patterns of the past shape the present and hint at the future. If we're paying attention, we'll see that history often repeats itself. Use that insight—not to remain trapped in cycles, but to break them. Let vision guide your steps beyond what has already been.

Vision isn't prediction—it's perception. If tomorrow was yesterday and yesterday was today, then the future is written, and history has already spoken. This isn't just poetic—it's prophetic. It reminds us that time is not always linear. It loops. It echoes. And those echoes hold clues.

True vision requires more than seeing what's ahead. It demands you to understand what has come before. To recognize the patterns, the habits, the consequences. Vision is what happens when hindsight and foresight meet in the present moment with clarity. The wise don't just look forward—they look through. They study history, personal and collective. They ask, Where have these choices led us before? What road did this mindset pave last time? Because patterns unexamined become cycles repeated.

Vision is the ability to lead with awareness.

It says, "I've seen this story. I know how it ends—unless we change it." It's not trapped in what has been; it's informed by it. And with that awareness, it dares to imagine—and build—what hasn't yet existed. To have vision is to rise above the surface noise and zoom out. To stop reacting and start designing. Vision doesn't need full clarity—it just needs conviction. And it doesn't need certainty—it needs courage to move toward what's possible, even when others are still focused on what's been. Let the past be your blueprint—but not your ceiling. Let history inform your movement, not limit it. And when you see what others cannot, don't wait for agreement.

VALOR

The spoils of war go to those who serve, and to the cowards that hide, we offer the remains of the wretched.

True valor is found on the front lines—where sacrifice, loyalty, and courage converge. It honors those who step forward when others retreat. In times of struggle, comfort without contribution has no glory. Only those who serve boldly, with heart and action, earn the rewards that come from standing for something greater than themselves.

Valor isn't loud—it's lived. The spoils of war go to those who serve, and to the cowards that hide, we offer the remains of the wretched. It's a sharp truth: glory doesn't belong to those who observe, criticize, or stay in the shadows. It belongs to those who engage. Those who risk. Those who show up.

Valor is not about aggression or bravado. It's about standing firm in the face of fear—not because you're fearless, but because you've chosen to act anyway.

It's service with sacrifice, loyalty without spotlight, courage without conditions. We are often tempted to avoid discomfort, to choose the easier road, to protect ourselves from the heat of difficult moments. But valor asks more. It calls us to the front lines of our values, our convictions, our responsibilities.

It asks us to carry burdens that aren't ours because it's right. To speak up when silence is safer. To serve even when service goes unthanked. It's the nurse who stays during a storm. The parent who never quits. The leader who takes the hit first. The neighbor who intervenes. Valor is rarely dramatic—but it is always deliberate.

And while those who hide may stay comfortable, they will never know the reward of having stood. So if the battle comes to your door—whatever it may be—don't shrink. Because valor isn't found in avoiding the war. It's found in knowing who you fight for, why it matters, and choosing to fight with heart.

COURAGE

Get ready to do the things you fear to achieve the things you dare.

Dreams require more than hope—they demand bravery. Embrace discomfort and fear as necessary steps toward your goals. The life you dare to imagine is guarded by the very fears you hesitate to face. Step forward anyway. Courage doesn't erase fear—it overcomes it. Everything you want—the breakthrough, the freedom, the calling you can't stop thinking about—lives just on the other side of fear.

Get ready to do the things you fear to achieve the things you dare. Because the life you envision won't arrive wrapped in comfort. It arrives through confrontation—confrontation with your doubts, your hesitations, your belief that maybe you're not ready. But here's the truth: readiness isn't a feeling. It's a decision.

Courage is not the absence of fear. It's not about being fearless—it's about acting anyway.

It's standing in front of the unknown, feeling the tremble in your chest, and taking the step because the goal is worth it. Fear is loud, persuasive, and often disguised as logic. It will tell you to wait. To play safe. To avoid risk. But courage whispers back, "What if it works? What if it's your turn?" That whisper is the spark that changes everything.

Courage is choosing the hard conversation. Sending the application. Taking the leap. Saying "yes" when you're scared—and saying "no" when it's needed. It's doing the thing that your future self will thank you for, even if your present self is unsure.

The life you dare to dream won't just require your talent. It will demand your courage. Your willingness to step into spaces where fear says "stop"—and you say "go anyway." So breathe. Shake if you must. But take the step. Because courage doesn't guarantee success. But it guarantees movement. And movement is where everything begins.

LOVE

Bring love into your home and watch as evil is evicted.

Love is the ultimate cleanser of negativity. When nurtured and rooted at home, love has the power to banish resentment, pain, and darkness. It is not just an emotion; it's a presence that transforms space and heals wounds. Where love lives, fear cannot. Love is not passive. It is not timid. It is not simply a warm feeling or a poetic word. It is the most active, powerful, and transformative force we can welcome into our lives—and most importantly, into our homes.

Bring love into your home and watch as evil is evicted. The truth in that line runs deep. Love doesn't just brighten a room—it purifies it. It reshapes the tone of every conversation, every relationship, every silence. It doesn't merely coexist with darkness—it displaces it.

Evil doesn't always wear a mask. It can appear as bitterness, indifference, resentment, or emotional neglect. It lives in the cold distance between family members under the same roof. In unspoken tensions. In long-standing wounds never healed. But love—when it is truly practiced—has the power to call those things out without blame, and clear them out without violence.

Love brings safety. Not the kind of safety rooted in control, but in connection.

It allows people to be seen and known without fear. It makes room for vulnerability. It forgives before it's asked. It notices pain before it speaks. It speaks life into rooms that have gone quiet. And love starts with you. Not with perfection, but with intention. It begins in how you speak to your children, your partner, your parents. It lives in how you respond when anger flares, when disappointment hits, when silence lingers. Love doesn't require grand gestures—it requires presence. Eye contact. A patient tone. The willingness to say, "I was wrong." The courage to say, "I love you" without conditions.

Love is not just something you feel—it's something you choose. Daily. Especially when it's hard. Especially when it's easier to retreat into frustration or isolation. And the beauty of love is that once it's planted, it grows. One seed of love can soften generations of hardness. One act of love can shift an entire atmosphere. One moment of love—real, unguarded, unselfish—can set someone free.

So start where you are. Water the space around you with kindness. Be the one who brings light into the room. Be the one who says the hard truth with soft eyes. Be the one who chooses reconciliation over righteousness. Because when love is rooted at home, it becomes a fortress. And where love is established, anything that threatens peace—be it fear, pride, hatred, or pain—cannot stay. Love is not just the answer. It is the environment in which all answers can be heard.

CONVICTION

If fate brings you chaos, don't turn and run; face it with the power of conviction.

L ife won't always be kind, but conviction gives you the strength to stand firm. Inner resolve holds you steady when the ground shakes. With conviction, you don't need guarantees—you need purpose. When chaos comes, let your beliefs anchor you and your courage drive you forward. Chaos has a way of revealing who we are beneath the surface. When everything is spinning, when certainty disappears, and when fear rises, we are stripped of convenience—and faced with truth.

If fate brings you chaos, don't turn and run; face it with the power of conviction. Because when the storm comes, you don't need to have all the answers. You just need to remember what you believe in. Conviction isn't about being rigid—it's about being rooted. It's the deep inner alignment that says, "This is who I am. This is what I stand for." It's what keeps your soul grounded when your surroundings fall apart.

In the face of uncertainty, conviction gives you clarity. In the face of noise, it gives you direction. It's the power that holds your gaze when the world tries to distract you, the strength that helps you speak when silence is safer, and the resilience that gets you back up when everything says stay down.

Conviction turns hesitation into movement. Not because the path is easy, but because the purpose is real.

To live with conviction is to stop waiting for conditions to be perfect before you act. It's to choose meaning over comfort. Purpose over popularity. Integrity over ease. And when you move with that kind of resolve—when you face chaos with your values intact—you don't just survive. You shape what happens next. So let the winds come. Let the ground tremble. Conviction doesn't ask the world to make sense. It simply stands—so others remember how.

LEADERSHIP

In the absence of many, the one with the strongest voice rules the day.

L eadership isn't always assigned—it's often assumed. In moments of uncertainty or silence, the boldest voice becomes the guiding force. True leadership emerges not from titles, but from courage, clarity, and presence. When others falter or fade, step forward. Your voice might be the one that leads the way. Leadership is not a position—it's a posture.

In the absence of many, the one with the strongest voice rules the day. Not because they're louder, but because they're willing. Because they stepped forward when others hesitated. Because they chose direction over delay, service over status, and responsibility over retreat. True leadership often arises in moments no one prepared for. It shows up when the plan falls apart. When people are scared. When vision is clouded and voices are quiet. It's in those moments that real leaders reveal themselves—not with titles, but with presence.

The strongest voice isn't always the one with the most volume—it's the one with the most conviction.

The one that speaks with clarity in the fog. The one that makes space for others to be heard. The one that says, "We may not have all the answers, but I'm willing to help find the way." Leadership isn't about knowing everything. It's about carrying something. A belief. A standard. A sense of responsibility for more than just yourself. It's about being visible when things go wrong—not just when they go right. It's about making hard decisions, owning your mistakes, and raising the bar without needing applause.

Sometimes, leadership will ask you to walk alone first—so others feel safe to follow. Sometimes, it will ask you to sit down so someone else can rise. Always, it will ask you to lead with integrity, not ego. So if you find yourself in a room where no one knows what to do next, don't wait for someone to tell you it's your turn. Start leading. Not because you're the loudest, but because you're the most ready to serve.

VALUES

Pick a color; any color, pick a number; any number, pick a time; any time, but always end on your values.

L ife offers infinite choices, but your values are the compass that keeps you grounded. While the world tempts us with variety and distraction, we must always return to what we believe in. Your values define your path, your purpose, and your integrity—never trade them for convenience. The world offers you choices—countless paths, shiny distractions, promises of speed and ease. Every day you are invited to reinvent yourself, reshape your image, or reframe your truth for the sake of convenience or applause.

Pick a color; any color, pick a number; any number, pick a time; any time... but always end on your values. Because when all the options fade, when the hype settles and the noise quiets, your values are what will remain. Values aren't about popularity—they're about identity. They're the things you stand on when everything else shifts. They're your core truths, unbothered by trends, untouched by pressure. They don't shout—they anchor. And that's why they're non-negotiable.

A world without values is a world of wandering.

Decisions become inconsistent. Standards blur. We say yes when we should say no, and stay quiet when our convictions should speak. Without values, we move—but we don't progress. Values aren't about being right. They're about being rooted. They protect your integrity when no one is watching. They inform your actions when you're under fire. They help you make decisions you can live with—long after the moment has passed.

The truth is, you will be tempted to compromise them. You'll be told to pick what's easier, faster, more profitable. But ease without alignment is emptiness. Speed without direction is chaos. So live loud—but live aligned. Choose freely—but choose wisely. Experiment with your interests, your style, your ideas—but return, always, to what you believe in. Because values aren't just your foundation—they're your filter. And in a world full of choices, the clearest path is the one that leads back to you.

GRATITUDE

To those that serve, we salute you; to those that try, we thank you; and to those failing to acknowledge the sacrifice, the commitment, and courage of others, we, we, we, we um; and tomorrow, we are stronger.

G ratitude is both a gesture and a legacy. Not all appreciation is spoken—but it must be felt. Even when thanks go unspoken, honor still rises. Gratitude builds bridges, binds communities, and strengthens resolve. Acknowledgment fuels service, and service builds the future. Gratitude is more than good manners. It's memory. It's acknowledgment. It's a quiet bow of the soul in the direction of those who gave—when they didn't have to.

To those that serve, we salute you; to those that try, we thank you... Gratitude is layered. It's for the warrior and the worrier. For those who lead from the front and those who hold us up from behind the scenes. For those who show up not for praise, but because it's right.

Gratitude, when practiced well, becomes more than a moment—it becomes a culture.

It becomes a current that pulls people together. It tells those who sacrifice, "You are seen." It tells those who struggle, "You matter." And it tells the indifferent, "You don't get to ignore the work others do to make your world turn." It's true—not everyone expresses thanks. Some avoid it. Some forget. Some choke on it because it means admitting they needed someone else. But that doesn't stop the need for gratitude. In fact, it amplifies it. Because silence toward service is a slow erosion of honor.

Gratitude isn't just about words—it's about perspective. It's what keeps the heart soft and the spirit lifted. It's what turns duty into devotion. It transforms labor into legacy. And most importantly, it strengthens us—collectively. Because when we express gratitude, we not only bless those who gave—we remind ourselves that we belong to one another. That no one climbs alone. That behind every success is a thousand small acts of support, courage, and unseen service. So say thank you. Out loud. Often. And if the words won't come—let your life be the thank you. Because gratitude doesn't just honor the past—it shapes the future.

GUIDANCE

When your eye needs vision, seek higher ground; when your heart needs direction, seek a higher power.

We all face moments of uncertainty. When clarity escapes us, perspective and faith can provide direction. Look above your circumstances to find your vision; look within and beyond for deeper purpose. Guidance often comes when we rise above our doubts and listen to what calls us forward. There are moments in life when our vision blurs—not because our eyes fail us, but because the path is crowded with noise, fear, and conflicting voices. In these moments, the next step feels uncertain, and the horizon seems too far away to find.

When your eye needs vision, seek higher ground; when your heart needs direction, seek a higher power.

These words are not about religion alone—they're about elevation. About choosing to rise above the overwhelm and reconnect with a perspective that's wider, deeper, and more grounded than the chaos at your feet. Higher ground offers clarity. It gives you space to breathe, to look at the big picture, and to realign with what matters most. And a higher power—however you define it—anchors your soul when your emotions are unstable. It reminds you that you're not alone in the uncertainty, and that guidance is never out of reach.

Often, we search for direction through noise—scrolling, asking everyone else, chasing answers outside ourselves. But real guidance comes when we pause. When we turn inward. When we allow silence to stretch long enough for insight to surface. Sometimes, guidance arrives as a whisper. Other times, as a tug on your spirit. And sometimes, it comes through detours that feel like delays—but are actually redirection.

To find your way forward, you must first rise above your doubts. Step back from your urgency. Ask for clarity—not just from the world, but from within. And when the way becomes clear, trust it. Because guidance doesn't always light the whole path—it simply shines enough light for the next step. Take that step.

COMPASSION

How great is the opportunity to serve others, especially those unable to serve themselves.

C ompassion is more than kindness—it's purposeful action. Real greatness lies in our willingness to serve. When we lift up the vulnerable, we strengthen humanity as a whole. Serving those who cannot repay us is not weakness—it's the purest expression of strength. We often measure greatness by influence, wealth, or recognition. But real greatness isn't found in spotlight moments—it's found in quiet acts of compassion.

How great is the opportunity to serve others, especially those unable to serve themselves. Not because it earns you points, but because it reveals who you are when no one is watching. Compassion is love made visible. It's the intentional act of noticing someone else's need and deciding to do something about it.

It's easy to be kind when it's convenient. It's easy to give when the return is guaranteed. But true compassion exists where there is no transaction—only care. It shows up for the overlooked, the unheard, the tired, the forgotten. Not out of pity, but out of respect. Not from above, but alongside. To serve someone who cannot repay you is to acknowledge their humanity—and your own. It's a declaration that everyone matters, regardless of what they can offer in return.

Compassion isn't weakness. It's strength refined.

It's the kind of strength that chooses empathy over ego, humility over hierarchy, and presence over productivity. And the impact? It ripples. One small act of compassion—holding a hand, listening without judgment, extending help—can shift someone's entire world. It can remind them they're not invisible. It can plant hope where there was only survival. So when the moment comes to act, take it. Not for applause. Not for credit. But because you can. Because every time we choose compassion, we don't just change lives—we honor them. And that is greatness.

OPPORTUNITY

A spark is the only thing needed for genuine opportunities to burst into existence.

Opportunities often begin in moments that seem small, even insignificant. The right spark—an idea, a conversation, or a choice—can ignite transformation. Stay open, stay ready. When passion meets preparation, even the faintest flicker can light the way to something extraordinary. We imagine opportunity as something grand—a spotlight moment, a door flung open, an obvious invitation. But more often, opportunity is subtle. It arrives quietly, disguised as inconvenience, uncertainty, or even failure.

A spark is the only thing needed for genuine opportunities to burst into existence. One spark. One idea. One unexpected meeting. One risk taken when it would've been easier to wait. That's how transformation begins—not with thunder, but with a flicker.

The thing about opportunity is, it rarely looks like what we expect. It doesn't always arrive in perfect packaging. Sometimes it comes in the form of disruption. Sometimes it's hidden inside rejection. Some-times, it's the moment when everything seems to fall apart—and that crack in the plan lets something entirely new begin. But you must be ready. You must be watching.

Opportunity favors the alert, the prepared, the willing.

Not necessarily the most talented or the most connected—but the most awake. The ones who stay curious, the ones who keep moving forward even when progress feels invisible. And when passion meets preparation—when your work, your heart, and your timing align—that's when sparks turn into wildfires. That's when possibility takes shape and what once felt distant becomes real. So trust the spark. Protect it. Feed it. And when it arrives, don't hesitate. Fan it into flame. Because your next chapter might be hiding in what looks like a whisper.

REBIRTH

When the walls of tyranny crumble, a new era emerges where peace and prosperity prevail.

Rebirth is a testament to renewal through resistance. It often follows collapse, as outdated systems give way to freedom and progress. Whether in societies or within us, transformation begins when old barriers fall. From ruin rises the opportunity to rebuild—stronger, freer, and more just. Rebirth never comes easy. It requires disruption. It demands the destruction of what no longer serves, no longer fits, no longer reflects who we are or who we're becoming.

When the walls of tyranny crumble, a new era emerges where peace and prosperity prevail. Whether we're talking about oppressive systems or personal strongholds, true transformation is often preceded by collapse. By the breaking of what once felt unbreakable.

Rebirth is the sacred process of becoming again—this time with greater intention, more awareness, and deeper strength.

It is not the same as starting over—it's starting from truth. Sometimes, what falls apart was never built to last. Sometimes, the systems that kept you comfortable were quietly keeping you confined. And sometimes, the end of one thing is the only way another can begin. Whether in a society seeking justice, a soul seeking freedom, or a person stepping into a new identity, rebirth is the promise that from ruin, we rise. But rising isn't passive. It's work. It's healing. It's reckoning with the pieces of who you were and deciding what deserves to return and what must be left behind.

Rebirth asks you to imagine something better—even while standing in the rubble. It asks you to rebuild, not in haste, but in wisdom. With clarity. With hope. It invites you to reclaim what was stolen. To recreate what was broken. To rise—not as who you were, but as who you've grown into. So when things crumble—internally or externally—don't rush to cover the cracks. Let them breathe. Because in that space of release, something greater is waiting to be born.

Inspiration

When everything is on the line, leaders are born, and inspiration will surely rise.

C risis reveals character. The moment pressure forges greatness, true leaders don't wait for comfort—they rise when it matters most. And in doing so, they inspire others to rise with them. Let urgency spark your strength and let that strength light the way for others. Inspiration is not born in quiet times—it is forged in fire. When everything is on the line, leaders are born, and inspiration will surely rise. These aren't just words for difficult seasons—they are a truth for every human being who finds themselves staring down fear, fatigue, or impossibility and decides to stand up anyway.

Inspiration doesn't always feel like light. Sometimes, it's a flicker in the dark—a fragile but determined force that whispers, "Keep going." It doesn't always begin with clarity or confidence. It often begins with a choice: to move, to speak, to show up—not because you're ready, but because it's needed.

True inspiration is born the moment someone rises while everything else falls.

When someone holds their ground in the face of pressure. When someone sacrifices comfort for conviction. These moments change more than circumstances—they change people. They spark courage in those watching silently, waiting for someone else to move first. And that's the beautiful tension of inspiration: it's not just for you. When you rise, you don't just lift yourself—you give others permission to do the same. Your resilience becomes a reference point. Your actions become a mirror that says, "You can do this too."

We often underestimate how inspiring we can be. We think we need big platforms, eloquent speeches, or perfect timing. But inspiration isn't always grand. Sometimes it's in how you show up for your family. How you fight for your healing. How you speak truth in love. How you carry yourself with grace under pressure. And it's not about being fearless. It's about being faithful. It's about holding the line when your knees shake. It's about staying committed to your mission, even when the odds scream quit.

Inspiration, at its core, is contagious integrity. It's what happens when belief is matched with action—when words are backed by presence, and presence turns into power. So don't wait for someone else to light the way. Be the spark. Rise—not for recognition, but because someone, somewhere, is watching and wondering if it's safe to rise too. Let your courage be the invitation. Let your resilience be the proof. Let your story become someone else's turning point. Because when everything is on the line, and you choose to rise, you don't just lead—you inspire.

MOTIVATION

Tell yourself what is needed to encourage the necessary thoughts; never fall short of one's imaginary powers.

The mind is a powerful ally—or a formidable opponent. Our self-talk shapes our reality. Feed your imagination with belief, and your actions will follow. Motivation isn't always external—it begins with the stories you tell yourself. Make them empowering. The most important voice you'll ever hear is the one in your own mind. Tell yourself what is needed to encourage the necessary thoughts; never fall short of one's imaginary powers. Because motivation is not something you wait for—it's something you build from within.

We often think we need the perfect speech, the perfect book, the perfect moment of clarity to feel motivated. But motivation doesn't start out there—it starts in here. It begins with the stories you tell yourself about what's possible, what you're capable of, and what you deserve. Your thoughts are not just passive—they are instructions to your brain. They tell your body how to act, your heart how to feel, and your future how to form. So what are you telling yourself? Because when you speak doubt, your actions shrink. When you speak fear, your effort stalls. But when you speak possibility, discipline, vision—your entire posture changes. You rise.

Motivation is not about feeling hyped every day.

It's about creating a mental environment that supports action—even on the hard days. It's the voice that says, "Try again." "Just do five more minutes." "You're stronger than this moment." And it doesn't have to be perfect. You don't need to be endlessly optimistic. You just need to be intentional. Shift one thought. Choose one better belief. Feed your imagination with words that align with the life you're trying to build. Because your imagination is not fiction—it's fuel. And your motivation is not found. It's formed—one empowering thought at a time.

FOUNDATION

The past is filled with introspections and is the building block and formation of sound strategies.

The future is built on lessons learned. Reflection is important—not to dwell, but to build wisely. Every misstep and every triumph contribute to a sturdier foundation. By understanding where we've been, we pave a more stable road ahead. Every tall structure begins beneath the surface. Every lasting success is anchored in what came before it. Before strategy can guide, vision can grow, or movement can gain momentum—there must be foundation.

The past is filled with introspections and is the building block and formation of sound strategies. Life doesn't begin with the future—it begins with reflection. With looking back not in shame, but with curiosity. Not with regret, but with reverence.

Your past is not something to escape. It's something to examine. Because within every mistake lies a message. Within every delay lies a decision. Within every heartbreak lies a hidden blueprint that shaped the strength you carry today. The foundation of your future isn't just formed by what you got right—it's forged by what you learned when everything fell apart. It's made of the lessons that emerged after disappointment. The realizations that surfaced after silence. The wisdom that came from sitting still long enough to ask, What did that season teach me?

> **Building a strong foundation doesn't mean avoiding pain—it means turning pain into perspective.**

It means understanding that strategy without reflection is fragile. That speed without depth is dangerous. And that success, when not grounded in experience, rarely sustains. And this applies to everything—your career, your relationships, your identity, your leadership. If you want to build something meaningful, it can't just be exciting—it has to be anchored.

So revisit your past—not to live there, but to learn from it. Study your patterns. Honor your growth. Ask better questions. And use what you find to build something that lasts. Because when the winds come—and they will come—it's not your dreams that will hold you steady. It's your foundation.

CHARITY

Kindness is a power that fuels those with the gift of selfless service.

Charity is not only about giving—it's about empowering. It honors the quiet strength of those who serve without expectation. True charity uplifts both giver and receiver. In a world full of need, those who give from the heart become beacons of hope and healing. Charity is not a transaction. It's a transmission of humanity.

Kindness is a power that fuels those with the gift of selfless service. That power isn't loud. It doesn't need recognition. But it moves through people with quiet authority—softening hearts, restoring dignity, and planting hope in places long abandoned. True charity isn't just the act of giving—it's the heart behind the giving. It's not about how much you give, but how you give.

When you serve without expecting anything in return, you turn a simple gesture into a sacred one. And in that exchange, something transformative happens: the giver is strengthened as much as the receiver. Because charity does not deplete—it multiplies. It multiplies trust, compassion, courage. It ripples outward into communities, relationships, and lives we may never directly see. That's the beauty of selfless service—it leaves an imprint that often outlives the moment.

In a world often driven by what we can gain, charity asks, what can I offer?

In a culture obsessed with status, charity elevates service. And in times of division and scarcity, charity becomes a bridge—a quiet declaration that we are still connected, still responsible for one another. So don't wait until you have extra. Give when it's inconvenient. Give when it's unnoticed. Give with your time, your attention, your presence. Sometimes, what people need most isn't your money—it's your willingness to care. Because when charity flows from the heart, it does more than meet needs. It heals.

VICTORY

Five years of theory, nine months to prepare, seven days of battle for one moment of victory.

Victory is rarely spontaneous—it is the culmination of preparation, endurance, and unwavering belief. The timeline of triumph reminds us that the journey is long and demanding. That final moment of success is brief, but its value is earned through every second of the process. Prepare, persist, and let your moment shine.

Victory is not just a moment—it's a legacy built in silence. Five years of theory, nine months to prepare, seven days of battle for one moment of victory. That moment—the one where the crowd erupts, the weight lifts, or the door finally opens—may last only seconds. But behind it lies a thousand small decisions, countless sacrifices, and a commitment that outlasted convenience.

We often romanticize winning. We see the medals, the applause, the outcome. But what we rarely acknowledge is how much of the journey is invisible. The nights spent in quiet discipline. The days filled with doubt. The setbacks that made you question everything, and the internal pep talks that no one else ever heard. Victory begins long before the world recognizes it. It begins when you decide that your dream is worth the cost. That the process is worth the pain. That success is not about arriving quickly—it's about becoming ready to handle what you've been working for.

Theory builds knowledge. Preparation builds strength. Battle builds character.

And victory? Victory proves that it was all worth it—not because of the trophy, but because of who you had to become in order to claim it. And even then, the win is not the end. It's the result of a process that shaped you. And it's often only the beginning of what you're truly capable of. That's why the most powerful victories are earned, not given. They are built in isolation and revealed in the light. They are forged in failure, refined in effort, and sealed by persistence.

So prepare well. Work in the shadows. Take the loss. Learn the lesson. Sharpen your tools. Stay the course. Because the ones who rise to meet their moment are the ones who never stopped building toward it—even when the moment felt far away. And when that moment arrives, it won't just be a celebration. It will be confirmation that every step, every scar, and every sacrifice led you exactly where you were meant to be.

DEVOTION

Greatness can be measured by a king and his subjects but can easily be identified by a mother and her unwavering love.

D evotion is not always loud or royal—it is often quiet, enduring, and deeply personal. It honors the unparalleled strength of a mother's love. True greatness doesn't seek a throne; it offers care, protection, and sacrifice day after day. In devotion, we find the purest form of leadership and love. Greatness doesn't always wear a crown. Sometimes, it wears tired eyes and gentle hands.

Greatness can be measured by a king and his subjects but can easily be identified by a mother and her unwavering love.

That's because true devotion doesn't need a title. It doesn't need applause. It exists not for status, but for service. Devotion is a daily decision. It's waking up and choosing to give, even when you're empty. It's staying up late to comfort, protect, provide, and love—again and again, without recognition, without asking for anything in return.

In the context of a mother's love, devotion takes on its highest form. It is unconditional. Unshakable. Sacrificial. And often unseen. It builds lives, shapes futures, and holds families together. Yet it rarely receives the honor it deserves. But devotion isn't about visibility. It's about presence. The kind that endures through hardship, stays steady in chaos, and remains faithful even when it goes unnoticed.

And it's not limited to mothers. Devotion is found in mentors, caregivers, teachers, protectors—anyone who loves with their actions and leads with their heart. It is in the friend who never leaves, the partner who shows up, the stranger who serves out of compassion rather than credit.

In a world driven by ego and applause, devotion is revolutionary. It says, "I am here not to be praised, but to be present. Not to be served, but to serve. Not for glory, but for love." That's greatness. And when you live with that kind of devotion—consistent, humble, unwavering—you may never sit on a throne. But you will move mountains.

ADAPTABILITY

When life gives you apples, crush them and make apple pie; but when life gives you grapes, make wine and have a grand time.

Adaptability is about embracing change with creativity and joy. It encourages us to take what we're given and turn it into something meaningful—or even delightful. Life won't always go as planned, but that's not a barrier; it's an invitation to innovate, celebrate, and thrive.

Adaptability is among humanity's greatest tools for survival and progress. Throughout history, it is adaptability—not strength alone—that has allowed civilizations, organizations, and individuals to flourish despite drastic changes or difficult circumstances. Consider inventors whose creations often emerged not from ideal conditions but out of necessity and improvisation. They recognized unexpected setbacks as opportunities for innovation rather than as signs to abandon their efforts. Similarly, entrepreneurs frequently thrive by responding quickly and creatively to shifting market conditions, turning potential threats into new opportunities.

On a personal level, adaptability asks us to shift our perspective from rigidly adhering to one vision toward welcoming new possibilities.

A sudden career change, the loss of a loved one, or unforeseen health challenges all initially feel devastating, yet often provide pathways for personal growth, deeper understanding, or the discovery of new passions. Adaptability enables individuals to move beyond mere coping, instead transforming disruption into fuel for creativity and joy.

To cultivate adaptability, practice viewing setbacks as puzzles rather than barriers. Regularly challenge yourself by learning new skills, embracing diverse experiences, or exploring unfamiliar environments. Over time, you'll find yourself responding to uncertainty with a sense of curiosity and creativity rather than anxiety or resistance. Ultimately, the adaptable mindset enriches your life's journey, converting every unexpected circumstance into an opportunity to build resilience, create meaning, and experience joy.

FORTITUDE

Patience is your strongest ally, only second to the power of faith.

F ortitude is quiet strength—the ability to endure while waiting for the right moment. Patience, when rooted in faith, becomes a powerful force. It holds us steady in storms and fuels us when hope runs low. Trust the timing and believe in the unseen work that's unfolding.

Fortitude is the enduring quality that underpins every meaningful achievement, whether personal, professional, or spiritual. More than mere endurance, fortitude integrates patience and faith into an inner resilience that thrives despite uncertainty and prolonged adversity. History honors individuals of fortitude—leaders who guided nations through turmoil, scientists who persisted through repeated failures, artists who tirelessly refined their craft until their vision was realized. Their greatest strength was not just their talent or knowledge, but their ability to hold firm and maintain conviction when faced with obstacles or delay.

Imagine an individual working years toward a major personal goal, such as completing advanced education or mastering a complex skill. Early enthusiasm inevitably faces periods of doubt, fatigue, and frustration. Fortitude, however, encourages patience during these difficult times by reminding them that meaningful outcomes often demand sustained effort over extended periods. This patience isn't passive waiting—it is active, intentional, disciplined persistence rooted deeply in the belief that eventually, their efforts will bear fruit.

Faith complements patience by offering confidence in a positive outcome even without immediate evidence.

Faith here might be spiritual, trusting in a higher purpose, or simply confidence in oneself or one's community. Fortitude, therefore, is the intersection of these elements: it's patience reinforced by faith, creating a powerful internal anchor that holds steady during life's most turbulent storms.

To develop fortitude, cultivate habits that nurture patience and faith—practicing mindfulness, daily reflection, setting long-term goals, and consistently reminding yourself of your purpose and values. By doing so, fortitude becomes second nature, turning seemingly insurmountable obstacles into manageable challenges. Ultimately, fortitude ensures that when the right moment arrives, you're fully prepared to seize it—precisely because you've patiently and faithfully endured.

PEACE

In my sanctuary, time is irrelevant, only relaxation matters.

P eace isn't found in the absence of time but in freedom from urgency. It reflects the serenity of a personal sanctuary—a space where clocks don't dictate, and pressure disappears. True peace is when you feel fully present, unbothered, and whole. Seek that space, and let it restore you.

Peace is not merely the absence of conflict or noise, but a deliberate creation of tranquility within ourselves. Imagine your personal sanctuary: a place or state of being where external stresses and internal worries lose their power. In this sanctuary, time is not measured by ticking clocks or looming deadlines, but by deep breaths, quiet moments, and genuine calm. Whether it's a physical location—a cozy room, a garden, a quiet corner—or an internal mindset achieved through meditation or mindfulness practices, this space is yours alone, shielded from the demands of the outside world.

In modern life, we are constantly bombarded with demands for our attention. Work obligations, family responsibilities, digital distractions—each of these vies relentlessly for our energy, pulling us away from inner serenity. True peace arises when we consciously withdraw from this chaos, not to escape permanently but to replenish ourselves.

In your sanctuary, urgency evaporates, allowing you to fully engage with the present moment.

This sense of presence helps reset your mental clarity, emotional balance, and spiritual alignment. Achieving such peace requires intention and discipline. Schedule time regularly to disconnect from technology, silence notifications, and step away from routines. Allow yourself the luxury of stillness, recognizing it not as idle inactivity but as essential restoration. Over time, these purposeful pauses will foster a resilient inner peace that remains accessible even in the midst of external turmoil, empowering you to face life's challenges with composure and clarity.

RESILIENCE

Anticipate life's challenges so the power of defeat becomes meaningless.

R esilience isn't just about bouncing back—it's about being ready before the storm hits. Preparing mentally, emotionally, and spiritually for life's inevitable obstacles allows you to show up with strength. When you expect the struggle and still press forward, defeat loses its grip. Anticipation builds strength, and strength makes resilience second nature.

True resilience goes beyond recovery after setbacks; it involves actively preparing yourself before hardships arrive. This proactive approach involves cultivating mental toughness, emotional intelligence, and spiritual fortitude long before adversity strikes. When life inevitably throws obstacles your way—whether unexpected financial hardship, personal loss, or professional setbacks—you're not taken by surprise, but instead, you respond instinctively with strength and determination.

Anticipation is the cornerstone of resilience.

Much like an athlete rigorously trains for competition, resilience requires consistent mental and emotional conditioning. Imagine life's challenges not as threats but as inevitable training grounds for growth and development. Each anticipated hardship becomes an opportunity to build capacity, to refine coping mechanisms, and to strengthen your resolve. By visualizing potential challenges and planning how you'll handle them, you diminish their power to overwhelm you.

Moreover, spiritual resilience plays a vital role, offering a deeper foundation of purpose and meaning to withstand life's pressures. Believing in a larger purpose or aligning your actions with core values transforms your perspective on setbacks. Rather than viewing them as personal failures, you see them as opportunities for growth and deeper understanding.

To cultivate resilience, routinely practice mental and emotional exercises such as positive visualization, reflective journaling, and mindful meditation. Learn from every experience—both your own and others'—and integrate those lessons into future preparations. Over time, you'll find yourself increasingly unshakable, confidently navigating challenges and reducing the psychological impact of defeat, turning every struggle into a stepping stone toward personal empowerment and lasting strength.

Awareness

To improve one's perspective, one must embrace a listening strategy.

A wareness begins with listening—not just hearing but truly understanding. Perspective is expanded not by talking, but by receiving. When we tune into others' stories, pain, and wisdom, we sharpen our own insight. Listening opens the door to growth, empathy, and enlightened decision-making.

Genuine awareness involves deep listening—a conscious, purposeful act far beyond merely hearing words. Active listening requires humility, openness, and curiosity. It means setting aside personal biases, preconceived notions, and the urge to interject, allowing space for another's thoughts, emotions, and experiences to fully emerge. In doing so, your own perspective grows broader and richer, colored by the diverse insights gleaned from those around you.

Awareness shaped through listening transforms interactions.

Whether with family members, colleagues, or complete strangers, when we listen deeply, we acknowledge the validity of their experiences. This simple acknowledgment fosters trust, encourages vulnerability, and opens pathways for genuine dialogue and mutual understanding. Over time, it nurtures empathy, allowing you to experience life from multiple viewpoints, enriching your capacity for compassion and informed decision-making.

Moreover, listening extends beyond interpersonal interactions into self-awareness. Regularly taking time to listen inward—reflecting on your own emotions, thoughts, and reactions—deepens your understanding of yourself. You learn what motivates you, what drains you, and where your true strengths lie. This heightened internal awareness allows you to respond rather than react, choose deliberately rather than impulsively, and lead authentically.

To enhance your listening skills, practice active listening in conversations by maintaining eye contact, acknowledging the speaker, and asking meaningful follow-up questions. Regularly reflect on what you hear and how it aligns with or challenges your own beliefs. With time, you'll find your perspective becoming clearer, richer, and more inclusive, guiding you toward more thoughtful and impactful interactions and decisions.

ADVENTURE

Plan a trip to nowhere and find yourself traveling everywhere.

Sometimes, the best journeys are the ones without a destination. Adventure is about embracing the experience—not chasing an end. Let curiosity lead, let expectations go, and you may discover more than you ever intended. Freedom, discovery, and transformation lie in the unplanned.

An adventure defined by spontaneity invites unexpected revelations and personal growth. When you set aside detailed itineraries, you open yourself up to opportunities you could never have anticipated. Imagine stepping onto a path without knowing precisely where it leads, guided instead by a sense of wonder and excitement for the unknown. Such journeys teach you more about yourself than any carefully planned trip ever could.

**Adventure in its purest form is the embodiment
of embracing uncertainty.**

It forces you out of comfort zones, challenging your resilience, adaptability, and courage. When you stop measuring success by reaching predetermined destinations, every moment becomes a destination in itself—rich with lessons, relationships, and insights. A journey without a fixed point can reconnect you to a sense of presence often lost in daily routines, urging you to savor each experience and interaction.

Allow yourself to follow unmarked roads and engage with unfamiliar cultures, conversations, and landscapes. Adventure, when undertaken with an open heart, turns obstacles into thrilling detours, and the unfamiliar into welcoming discoveries. By releasing the urge to control every detail, you reclaim freedom, deepen your capacity for joy, and find transformation in every step taken into the unknown.

TRANSPARENCY

If your actions require darkness, they might not be worth undertaking. Shed light on evil and bring it to the surface.

I ntegrity thrives in the open. If something must be hidden, it deserves questioning. Transparency brings clarity, accountability, and trust. When you illuminate the truth—even the uncomfortable parts—you create a space where growth and justice can flourish. Let honesty be your filter.

Transparency is more than simply being open—it is the willingness to expose actions, intentions, and decisions to scrutiny, knowing that truth withstands examination. When actions demand secrecy or manipulation, they inherently betray a lack of integrity or potential harm. Genuine transparency requires bravery because it sometimes means confronting uncomfortable truths, acknowledging failures, and facing criticism openly.

By choosing transparency, you establish trust, foster accountability, and cultivate an environment where authenticity can thrive.

It transforms organizations, relationships, and even personal character, laying foundations for genuine collaboration and meaningful relationships. The choice to reveal rather than conceal creates an atmosphere where individuals feel safe to admit mistakes, learn openly from setbacks, and collaboratively find solutions.

Promoting transparency is a courageous act. It means holding yourself and others to standards of honesty that build lasting respect and credibility. By continuously practicing transparency, you strengthen moral clarity, make wiser decisions, and build cultures of fairness, justice, and integrity. The act of shining a light on hidden truths empowers you and those around you to confront issues head-on, ultimately paving the way toward meaningful progress.

RESPONSIBILITY

When ignorance is not a defense, you owe it to yourself to fight like it matters.

A ccountability begins when excuses end. We must take ownership of our actions and decisions, especially when the stakes are high. Ignorance may explain the past, but it cannot justify inaction. When you're called to rise, rise with purpose—because your effort, your fight, and your responsibility truly matter.

Responsibility is the cornerstone of personal and collective growth. It compels you to recognize the weight of your choices and the significance of your actions, especially when facing difficult or challenging situations. When ignorance is no longer acceptable, there is an imperative to seek knowledge, to educate yourself, and to engage actively in finding solutions rather than settling for passivity or complacency.

**To be responsible is to move beyond acknowledg-
ing your role—it's about demonstrating courage
and determination to act meaningfully and deliberately.**

Recognizing your responsibility fosters strength and maturity, prompting you to confront uncomfortable truths, right wrongs, and stand firm even when it would be easier to turn away. Responsibility does not burden; it empowers. It fuels purpose-driven action, transforming intentions into impacts and aspirations into realities.

True responsibility also means recognizing the ripple effect your actions have on others and the broader community. Taking ownership ensures you leave a legacy of positive change rather than unintended consequences. When the stakes are high, remind yourself of the power inherent in your response. By facing your challenges head-on and fighting for what's right and meaningful, you contribute to a culture of courage, accountability, and meaningful progress, ultimately inspiring others to follow your lead.

REFLECTION

When faced with a problem, remember solutions aren't formed without reflection.

Every solution begins in stillness. Quick fixes rarely lead to deep answers. It is through thoughtful reflection that clarity emerges. Step back, consider the bigger picture, and let your mind settle. In that space of pause, real wisdom finds its voice.

Reflection is a powerful, yet often overlooked, tool in problem-solving. When you encounter challenges, your first instinct might be to act swiftly. However, true clarity and lasting solutions arise when you intentionally pause, stepping away from immediate pressures to thoughtfully examine the core of the issue. This period of reflection provides space for your thoughts to mature, enabling a deeper understanding of underlying causes and potential consequences.

Through reflection, you move beyond surface-level reactions.

It encourages you to explore various perspectives, possibilities, and outcomes, transforming instinctive responses into well-considered decisions. Reflection demands patience but rewards you with insights you wouldn't otherwise attain. It enhances self-awareness, strengthens critical thinking, and refines your judgment.

Integrating reflection into your decision-making processes elevates your ability to learn from experience and prepare better for future challenges. Ultimately, reflection shapes you into someone who responds to life's complexities not just effectively, but wisely—guiding you toward answers that stand the test of time.

GRATITUDE

When life throws you a battlefield, be prepared for war; when life exposes you to drama, be grateful it's not an act of war.

Perspective is powerful. While life may present chaos, we must measure our response. Not every challenge is a catastrophe. Be grateful when the battle is metaphorical and not fatal. Recognize the difference and honor the peace you do have—however small it may seem.

Gratitude is more than simply being thankful—it is a deliberate choice to find value in each experience, regardless of its nature. Life inevitably delivers battles, both small and significant.

By intentionally practicing gratitude, you cultivate resilience and the strength to maintain composure even when surrounded by turbulence.

Recognizing the difference between true crisis and manageable drama helps you maintain balance and perspective. The act of being grateful for lesser challenges prevents unnecessary anxiety and reinforces your emotional resilience. This practice trains your mind to appreciate relative peace, even amidst difficulties, rather than magnifying minor troubles into overwhelming burdens.

Incorporating gratitude into daily life enhances emotional well-being, enriches your relationships, and builds deeper personal fulfillment. Through gratitude, you acknowledge not just obvious joys but the subtle mercies and quiet victories within ordinary struggles. By intentionally reframing challenges as opportunities for learning and growth, gratitude becomes a profound source of strength and inner peace.

Growth

Make room for errors so that real progress can take root.

Perfection isn't the goal—evolution is. Growth depends on our willingness to stumble, adjust, and try again. Mistakes aren't signs of weakness; they are evidence of effort. When we embrace error as a teacher, we clear the path for meaningful, lasting progress to take hold.

Growth is fundamentally a messy and iterative process. It thrives in environments where mistakes are not merely tolerated but actively encouraged as essential components of advancement. Aiming for perfection is admirable, but true, sustainable progress is fueled by the ability to embrace imperfections, learning continuously from each attempt, successful or otherwise.

> **When you shift your perspective to see errors as vital teachers, you eliminate the fear of failure that often paralyzes progress.**

This mindset transforms setbacks into powerful catalysts for personal and professional development. It allows you to adapt more effectively, sharpening your skills and expanding your understanding with each obstacle you overcome.

Real growth requires humility—acknowledging what you don't know and courageously exploring those unknown spaces. By normalizing errors and celebrating the resilience that emerges from them, you create fertile ground for innovation, creativity, and deep personal transformation. Each misstep, when openly examined, holds valuable insights that ultimately shape stronger foundations for lasting success.

BALANCE

Keep looking forward, focusing on progress but remember to look back to avoid yesterday's failures.

Balance lives in perspective. Ambition must be paired with awareness. While we strive toward the future, we must carry the wisdom of the past. Looking back isn't regression—it's caution, it's insight. Move forward but never forget what shaped your steps.

Balance isn't about staying in the middle—it's about thoughtfully moving between two essential viewpoints: your vision for tomorrow and the lessons of yesterday. As you chase progress and growth, it's easy to overlook the value hidden in past experiences. But true advancement demands the humility to acknowledge past missteps and the wisdom to integrate their lessons into future decisions.

When you reflect on where you've been, you illuminate the path ahead, helping you recognize recurring patterns, pitfalls, and opportunities you might otherwise miss. Looking back provides you with a map—rich in detail and invaluable for navigating uncertainties.

Your past failures, viewed through the lens of wisdom, become guides, not barriers.

Balance requires intentionality—fostering the discipline to pause and assess periodically. This careful blend of forward-thinking optimism and retrospective caution ensures you move with confidence rather than blind enthusiasm. Embracing this balanced perspective, you transform previous setbacks into steppingstones, strengthening your resilience and enhancing your ability to achieve sustained, meaningful progress.

PUNCTUALITY

To be late is problematic, but to be absent is akin to failure.

Time is a silent measure of respect. Showing up—on time and prepared—is often the difference between being reliable and being forgotten. Punctuality signals commitment; absence signals disconnection. When you honor others' time, you also honor your word.

Punctuality is more than the mere act of arriving on schedule; it's a powerful testament to character, respect, and integrity. It silently communicates to others how deeply you value their presence, commitments, and time. Being consistently punctual demonstrates your reliability, enhances your professional and personal credibility, and establishes a foundation of trust.

In contrast, lateness or absence doesn't just inconvenience—it subtly erodes relationships, diluting trust and confidence others have in you. Each time you fail to show up, you risk damaging your reputation and weakening the bonds you've cultivated.

Punctuality, therefore, is a reflection of your internal discipline, awareness, and accountability.

By treating punctuality as a non-negotiable personal standard, you set yourself apart as someone dependable, conscientious, and respectful. Your punctuality sends a clear message: your commitments matter, and you take them seriously. This mindful respect for others' time will lead to deeper, more reliable connections and greater success in all your endeavors.

CHAOS

In the absence of leadership, a void is created, and chaos will rain.

Where leadership falters, confusion rises. People crave direction, and when it's missing, disorder fills the space. Leadership isn't about control—it's about presence, clarity, and purpose. Step into the void, and you become the calm in someone else's storm.

Chaos emerges naturally wherever strong, purposeful guidance is missing. Human nature instinctively seeks structure and direction, making leadership a fundamental pillar of stable societies and effective groups. Yet, leadership does not necessarily mean wielding power or authority—it means providing clarity, stability, and a sense of direction during uncertainty.

In chaotic moments, people search for voices of reason, individuals who can illuminate a path out of confusion and turmoil.

When leadership is absent, the resulting void creates anxiety, conflicting visions, and disorganization. But within this very turmoil lies an opportunity for those willing to step forward with courage, authenticity, and vision. By choosing to lead, even in small moments, you become a force of calm and order amidst turbulence, instilling hope and direction where others might see only disorder. Your decisive presence becomes an anchor, transforming chaos into cohesion and uncertainty into unified purpose.

HAUNTED

When your shadow outpaces your steps, beware of the demons anchoring your feet.

Fear and doubt can move faster than we realize, casting shadows over our progress. When hesitation and past burdens hold us back, they grow stronger. The key is to confront them, not outrun them. Acknowledge what haunts you, face it with courage, and reclaim your steps. Being haunted isn't always about external ghosts—it's often about internal fears, past mistakes, and unresolved emotions that subtly but persistently follow you. These inner demons thrive in darkness, gaining strength from avoidance and denial. Like shadows stretching before you, they cast uncertainty over your path, causing hesitation, doubt, and stagnation.

True liberation begins with courageously turning toward what haunts you rather than away from it.

Face your fears honestly, examine your doubts critically, and confront your past compassionately. In doing so, you take away their power. These demons rely on your refusal to acknowledge them; once seen clearly, their control over your progress diminishes significantly.

By bravely addressing your internal obstacles, you reclaim agency over your life. Rather than being anchored by fear, guilt, or regret, you'll find newfound strength and clarity. Your shadow no longer dictates your direction—instead, your awareness and courage guide you forward toward growth, peace, and fulfillment.

ADAPTABLE

I am not a doctor, lawyer, teacher, or firefighter, but when trouble strikes, I adapt swiftly, and rise to the challenge.

Titles don't define capability—action does. Adaptability is the power to overcome obstacles through responsiveness and initiative. You don't need a specific role to be a problem solver. When challenges arise, resourcefulness and a willingness to learn will always position you ahead of those who wait for someone else to step in.

Adaptability transcends credentials, qualifications, or official titles. It's an innate strength, one that lies at the heart of resilience, success, and growth. Life is rarely predictable, and troubles arrive unannounced. Those who navigate change most effectively aren't necessarily the most trained—they are those who adapt quickly, responding with intelligence, flexibility, and creativity.

Being adaptable means thinking beyond the confines of your defined role and stepping boldly into situations that demand solutions.

This approach emphasizes action over hesitation, initiative over passive waiting, and creativity over conventional thinking. Your ability to rapidly assess changing circumstances, devise creative strategies, and implement solutions swiftly is what truly defines your capability—not a job description or professional title.

In moments of difficulty, adaptability becomes your greatest strength. By embracing challenges as opportunities to learn and innovate, you expand your capabilities and prove your value far beyond any predefined limits. With adaptability, you unlock a limitless potential, positioning yourself not just as a participant but as an essential problem-solver and a force of innovation wherever you go.

APATHY

Failing to try and trying to fail has one thing in common: a lack of motivation.

I naction and intentional failure are both rooted in the same thing: a loss of drive. The true enemy of progress isn't always defeat—it's indifference. The difference between success and stagnation lies in effort. The first step forward is choosing to care.

Apathy is more insidious than outright failure. At least failure results from effort and implies learning through experience. Apathy, however, extinguishes possibility before it ever begins. It silently corrodes ambition and diminishes potential, leaving talent unused, dreams unpursued, and goals unmet. Both the fear of trying and the intentional choice to fail stem from a loss of purpose and motivation, creating a cycle of stagnation and dissatisfaction.

True progress and fulfillment come from engage-ment, enthusiasm, and care.

Reigniting motivation requires acknowledging its absence and addressing the underlying cause—whether fear, doubt, or burnout. Rekindle your internal fire by reconnecting with your values, passions, and dreams. Remember why you began your journey and allow yourself to be inspired again. By choosing to care deeply and intentionally, you reclaim your momentum and re-establish your path toward growth, success, and fulfillment. The transformation from apathy to action is often the most powerful step toward positive change.

HINDRANCE

Yesterday's problems will always become a barrier to today's agenda.

H olding onto the past restricts today's growth. Unresolved issues don't disappear—they linger and obstruct progress. To move forward, we must clear the path. Whether it's regret, mistakes, or setbacks, release yesterday's burdens so today's opportunities can unfold.

A hindrance often arises from unresolved emotional baggage or lingering regrets from our past. When yesterday's issues are left unaddressed, they don't simply fade away—instead, they evolve into obstacles, clouding judgment, hindering creativity, and limiting effectiveness. Carrying unresolved problems from yesterday into today is like trying to run forward with heavy weights tied to your ankles; eventually, you'll find your momentum stalling, and progress becomes increasingly exhausting.

To break free from these hindrances, face them with honesty and courage.

Acknowledge mistakes, make peace with regrets, and commit to resolving unfinished business. Release resentment, forgive when necessary, and learn to accept what cannot be changed. Doing so clears emotional clutter, leaving mental space for innovation, productivity, and growth.

By letting go of yesterday's barriers, you allow today's possibilities to unfold freely. The path forward becomes clearer and lighter, enabling you to seize fresh opportunities without interference from outdated issues. Ultimately, by addressing past hindrances proactively, you pave the way for genuine progress, clarity, and sustained success.

IDENTITY

You were born with the sole purpose of being you.

There is no greater role to fill than your own. Your existence is not by accident, nor should it be an imitation of someone else. Your thoughts, experiences, and choices make you unique. Embrace them fully, for there is no one else who can be you but you.

Identity is your personal narrative, the unique story that only you can write. Your existence has purpose precisely because no one else shares your exact combination of talents, experiences, insights, and dreams. Society often pressures us to conform, to mirror others deemed successful, or to reshape our individuality to meet external expectations. Yet, in doing so, we dilute the authenticity that gives life its richest meaning. Your greatest strength is your individuality; it offers something to the world no one else can replicate.

True self-discovery requires courage. It demands a willingness to explore your passions, to embrace your flaws, and to cultivate your unique strengths.

Rejecting imitation is not about isolation or rebellion; it's about genuine self-expression. The moment you fully accept who you are, you liberate yourself to live a fulfilling life. Rather than chasing someone else's shadow, invest your energy in growing into the fullest version of yourself. Authenticity inspires trust, respect, and genuine connection with others. Ultimately, fulfilling your identity is not just your greatest achievement—it is your gift to the world.

SUBJECTIVE

Sacrifice carries various meanings, each shaped by individual biases.

W hat one person sees as noble, another may view as unnecessary. Perspectives on sacrifice are deeply personal, shaped by experience and belief. True understanding comes from recognizing that meaning is subjective—what you give up may not hold the same weight as someone else.

Sacrifice is inherently tied to our individual perceptions, beliefs, and values. The very definition of what constitutes sacrifice can differ dramatically from one person to the next. For one individual, giving up comfort or wealth to pursue a passion or help others might be considered a meaningful, enriching sacrifice. Another may perceive that same act as reckless or unnecessary. Our personal histories, cultural backgrounds, and deeply held beliefs color the lens through which we view every decision—especially those that require surrendering something valuable.

Recognizing subjectivity in sacrifice is critical for cultivating empathy and compassion.

Judgments about others' choices diminish when we understand that what feels significant or trivial to one might carry an entirely different emotional weight for another. Honoring this subjectivity means appreciating the complexity of human motivations and refraining from imposing a singular moral standard. Instead, true empathy involves attempting to see through others' eyes, even when their choices differ greatly from our own.

Understanding that sacrifice is subjective invites humility into our interactions. It encourages us to engage openly, ask questions, and listen without judgment. In doing so, we build bridges rather than walls, nurturing genuine connections founded on mutual respect and deeper comprehension of the diverse human experience.

SELF-SABOTAGE

When your emotions get in the way of your progress, you only have your feelings to blame.

Emotions can be powerful allies or dangerous obstacles. When we let fear, doubt, or frustration dictate our actions, we stall our own growth. Progress requires discipline, not just passion. Recognizing when emotions are holding us back is the first step to overcoming self-sabotage.

Self-sabotage is an internal struggle driven by emotions that derail our best intentions. Often subtle and insidious, it appears as procrastination, avoidance, or the persistent habit of second-guessing decisions. At its root lies fear—fear of failure, fear of success, fear of rejection—and these feelings become the invisible barriers preventing forward momentum. Our emotions, intended to enrich our lives, instead become obstacles when we allow them to dominate our thinking and actions without regulation.

Progress demands emotional intelligence—acknowledging and interpreting feelings without being controlled by them. Discipline is the bridge between emotional turmoil and purposeful action.

By recognizing self-sabotaging behaviors as emotional reactions rather than rational truths, we gain power over them.

This awareness gives us room to pause, reflect, and choose differently.

Overcoming self-sabotage requires a deliberate commitment to confront uncomfortable feelings directly rather than avoiding them. It means building resilience, setting boundaries, and cultivating self-awareness to redirect emotions constructively. When you master emotional discipline, your emotions shift from burdens to guides—empowering your decisions and fueling growth rather than hindering it. Ultimately, mastering your emotions is mastering your life.

SETBACK

Yesterday's problems always serve as obstacles to today's progress.

Old struggles don't vanish unless they're addressed. Unresolved issues will continue to slow forward movement. Progress requires clearing the debris of the past—learning from mistakes, closing unfinished business, and refusing to let yesterday's failures define today's efforts.

Setbacks are not isolated incidents; they are often cumulative, layered with remnants of past disappointments and unresolved conflicts. Like clutter that accumulates unnoticed, these unresolved issues build into barriers, creating persistent roadblocks that impede current endeavors. Ignoring yesterday's challenges rarely diminishes their power; instead, they quietly grow stronger, subtly influencing today's opportunities and tomorrow's outcomes.

Addressing setbacks is crucial to meaningful progress. It involves acknowledging past mistakes without becoming imprisoned by them.

It's essential to face these issues honestly and proactively, transforming them from lingering burdens into valuable lessons.

When we actively learn from setbacks, we cultivate wisdom, resilience, and strength, forging better strategies for future growth.

The most successful individuals do not merely overcome setbacks—they harness them as steppingstones toward greater clarity and capability. They know unresolved problems must be confronted, processed, and resolved, thereby freeing mental and emotional energy for more productive and forward-looking endeavors. Embrace setbacks as opportunities for refinement, not as definitive judgments of your worth. By resolving yesterday's conflicts, you clear your path for unobstructed progress today and build a more resilient foundation for tomorrow.

PURPOSE

Work demands effort to keep our spirit from drifting into the abyss of nothingness.

P urpose is what keeps us anchored. Without meaningful effort, we risk feeling lost or empty. Hard work isn't just about productivity—it's about fulfillment. When we engage in purposeful action, we find direction, motivation, and a deeper sense of worth.

Purpose is more than a mere concept—it's the gravitational force anchoring our existence. Without it, our efforts can feel hollow, repetitive, or pointless. When purpose is absent, our spirit begins to drift aimlessly, leaving us vulnerable to dissatisfaction, apathy, and existential unrest.

It's not just about earning a living or achieving milestones; purpose infuses our actions with

meaning, ensuring that every effort aligns with deeper personal values and aspirations.

To live purposefully means to embrace the challenging yet fulfilling journey of self-discovery. It means consciously identifying and pursuing what genuinely motivates and fulfills us, rather than following a predetermined path or the expectations of others. Purposeful work creates intrinsic satisfaction, offering not just material rewards but emotional and spiritual nourishment. It strengthens resilience, fuels motivation, and fosters a genuine sense of accomplishment, even amidst adversity.

When we lose sight of purpose, even success can feel empty. Conversely, when our actions are driven by purpose, even the simplest tasks gain significance. The smallest contribution feels impactful, the mundane becomes meaningful, and every step taken has clear intention. Cultivating purpose requires reflection, courage, and constant reassessment—asking not just what we do, but why we do it. Only through purposeful living can we fully anchor our spirit, preventing it from drifting into the void of meaninglessness.

RESOURCEFULNESS

A Koi fish in a shark pond will always have a winning strategy.

Survival isn't about strength alone—it's about adaptability. Intelligence, creativity, and resilience often outweigh brute force. In difficult situations, success comes not from overpowering the opposition, but from outmaneuvering it. Play smart, and you'll always find a way forward.

Resourcefulness transcends mere survival; it's the mastery of turning disadvantage into opportunity. The image of a koi fish thriving in a shark pond symbolizes how ingenuity, rather than raw power, becomes the key to thriving in seemingly impossible situations. The koi fish does not rely on size or strength—it relies on quick thinking, adaptability, and the ability to anticipate threats. It navigates challenges using cleverness and agility, qualities that outmatch brute force in the long run.

True resourcefulness involves looking beyond obvious solutions, adapting swiftly to changing circumstances, and thinking creatively under pressure.

It's about recognizing possibilities in limitations, opportunities in obstacles, and strengths in weaknesses. Resourceful people rarely feel trapped by circumstances; instead, they constantly seek alternative routes, innovative approaches, and strategic solutions.

Life is often a "shark pond"—filled with competition, unpredictability, and threat. But success belongs not to those who blindly fight every battle, but to those who know when to move forward, when to retreat, and when to pivot. Resourcefulness is the strategic advantage that allows individuals to flourish, regardless of environment or adversity. By embracing adaptability, nurturing creativity, and strengthening resilience, one can master the art of thriving in even the harshest waters.

STOICISM

If everything bothers you, you'll remain a bothered person. But if you choose not to be disturbed by anything, you'll remain unburdened by what has been.

Peace is a choice. Emotional turbulence often comes from within, not from the world around us. Learning to control reactions rather than external events is the essence of stoicism. When we detach from unnecessary distress, we gain freedom from past burdens and future anxieties.

Stoicism is not simply enduring life's hardships silently—it is actively mastering your emotional responses. It teaches that our inner peace is within our own control, shaped less by external events and more by our perception and interpretation of those events. When external circumstances control your emotional state, you become vulnerable, easily agitated, and constantly stressed. Stoicism, however, provides a protective shield, empowering you to choose serenity over chaos.

Practicing stoicism means embracing the principle that you cannot always control what happens around you, but you always have control over how you react.

It encourages acceptance of life's unpredictability, teaching us to detach from our impulsive reactions and judgments. When we master this emotional discipline, we remain calm amidst turmoil, steady amidst uncertainty, and resilient amidst adversity.

Choosing stoicism means consciously deciding what deserves your emotional energy and what doesn't. By doing so, you prevent past hurts and future worries from dictating your present peace. It is about adopting a mindset of purposeful neutrality and intentional calm. Stoicism thus transforms you from a victim of circumstances into the master of your own emotional well-being, cultivating a tranquility that is rooted deeply within.

TRUST

When building a strategy, belief in the process lays the foundation for success.

Success isn't just about planning—it's about trust. Faith in your strategy, your team, and yourself is crucial. Doubt weakens progress, but confidence reinforces it. A well-built foundation of belief ensures that even in uncertainty, the process moves forward.

Trust is the silent cornerstone of every successful endeavor. Strategies, no matter how carefully crafted, fall apart if not underpinned by genuine trust. When you believe in your plan, you act with confidence, clarity, and conviction. Such belief is contagious, inspiring teammates and partners to align with your vision and strengthen collective efforts.

However, trust is not blind faith—it's a calculated confidence that comes from thorough

preparation, clear understanding, and unwavering commitment to a shared vision.

It requires believing not just in the endpoint, but also in the steps and the people who will get you there. When challenges arise, it's this foundational trust that provides the strength to endure setbacks, adapt to changing circumstances, and persist even when immediate outcomes seem uncertain.

Building trust involves transparent communication, accountability, and consistency. These qualities cultivate reliability, making others feel secure and supported. A foundation built on trust holds firm even when tested by stress and pressure, while doubt creates cracks that widen under adversity. In essence, trust in your strategy, team, and yourself forms a cohesive bond, ensuring steady progress, resilience against obstacles, and ultimately, sustainable success.

RESILIENCE

A lie told is one rebuke owned; stay clear from lies and keep your conscience clear.

Resilience isn't just about enduring hardship—it's about carrying a clear conscience. Dishonesty creates inner turmoil and weakens resilience. Staying true to yourself and your values is the best way to weather life's challenges without regret weighing you down.

Resilience often conjures images of physical toughness or mental endurance, but at its deepest level, true resilience is intertwined with integrity. Every lie we tell adds weight to our minds, becoming an invisible burden, we carry forward. This internal struggle can weaken our resolve, distracting us from facing life's inevitable challenges head-on. When we compromise honesty, we erode self-trust, and the resulting internal discord makes it difficult to confidently withstand external adversity.

Choosing honesty—even when uncomfortable or inconvenient—is the cornerstone of genuine resilience.

A clear conscience strengthens your internal foundation, enabling you to withstand criticism, setbacks, and hardships with greater ease. Lies, on the other hand, trap you in a constant cycle of justification, explanation, and guilt, reducing your ability to rebound from difficulties.

Staying true to your values, especially under pressure, enhances your inner strength. Each truth you uphold becomes another pillar supporting your self-esteem, emotional well-being, and moral courage. A clear conscience does not mean perfection; rather, it means actively choosing honesty even in imperfect moments. Such transparency fortifies resilience, allowing you to face challenges unencumbered, free from regret and inner conflict.

CANDID

In your darkest hours, don't wait for allies—they rarely come running.

S trength comes from within, not from expectation. Waiting for rescue often leads to disappointment. When facing difficulty, self-reliance is the greatest ally. Those who find strength in solitude will never be left powerless, no matter who stands beside them.

To be candid is to embrace raw honesty about life's harsh realities—one of which is the solitude that often accompanies adversity. In difficult times, the instinct to wait for assistance or support from others is natural, yet too often we find ourselves alone when we need help the most. Recognizing this truth doesn't breed cynicism—it fosters independence and self-reliance.

The greatest strength is cultivated in solitude, not dependency. This inner strength becomes your most dependable ally, capable of weathering the darkest storms. Developing the ability to rely on your own judgment, resilience, and capabilities is empowering. It means you can navigate challenges confidently without waiting for validation or support that may never arrive.

However, cultivating this self-reliance does not imply isolation or distrust of others—it means prioritizing your inner resources first.

Allies and companions are valuable, yet the candid truth remains that in critical moments, the only certain source of strength lies within you.

Building a foundation of self-sufficiency enables you to appreciate help when it comes, without feeling helpless when it doesn't. This honest self-assessment fosters strength, courage, and authenticity, creating a resilience that stands independent of external circumstances.

EVOCATIVE

The first truth about humans is this: they are bound to their emotions, inseparable and relentless. And with that, let the conversation begin!

Emotions define human experience. We are not creatures of pure logic—we feel deeply, and that shapes our actions. Rather than resisting emotion, we must learn from it. Understanding ourselves and others begins with accepting that emotions drive the stories we live.

Humans are fundamentally emotional beings; every thought, action, and decision we make is tinted by the emotions we feel. Emotions color our perceptions, influence our relationships, and determine how we respond to life's situations. Far from being mere reactions, emotions reveal our deepest truths—what we value, what we fear, and what we love.

Rather than viewing emotions as a hindrance to rational thought, embracing them can provide profound insight.

Our emotional responses serve as internal guides, highlighting areas in our lives that need attention or change. Joy signals alignment, fear warns of potential danger, sadness reveals unmet needs, and anger can expose boundaries that have been crossed.

Accepting the role emotions play in our lives invites deeper self-awareness and enriches interpersonal relationships. When we recognize our emotions and allow ourselves to experience them fully, we create space for empathy, compassion, and genuine connection. Instead of suppressing feelings, learning to manage and interpret them equips us with powerful tools for navigating life's complexities. By accepting emotions as indispensable parts of the human condition, we begin more authentic, meaningful conversations with ourselves and those around us.

RESOLVE

Muster the courage to do the impossible and find your strength in the depths of uncertainty.

Greatness is found in the unknown. Facing the impossible with courage brings out true strength. It doesn't come from easy paths—it comes from walking through fear and doubt with unwavering resolve. When the way forward is unclear, conviction becomes the guiding force.

Resolve is the quiet determination that propels us forward, even when clarity is lacking, and doubt is ever-present. The essence of resolve lies in the willingness to confront uncertainty head-on, embracing the potential for failure yet continuing to move forward. Courage isn't the absence of fear—it's the deliberate decision to persist despite it.

True strength is often revealed not through easy victories but in the moments when success seems distant or unlikely. It surfaces when we refuse to retreat, when we choose to keep pushing despite obstacles, pain, and discouragement.

The resolve to pursue the impossible sets individuals apart, distinguishing dreamers from achievers, and wishful thinkers from those who realize greatness.

Cultivating resolve requires a clear sense of purpose and a deep-seated belief in one's potential. When uncertainty clouds your path, conviction becomes your compass, guiding your steps through the ambiguity. Each difficult step strengthens your determination, reinforcing the belief that no goal is beyond reach if pursued relentlessly. It is in the uncertain darkness where the brightest discoveries are made—about our capabilities, our limits, and our unwavering capacity for resilience and transformation.

GRIT

To excel at anything, one must persevere, endure pain, and push forward until that pain reveals a glimpse of greatness.

G rit is the difference between wishing and achieving. Success isn't about talent alone—it's about persistence through discomfort. Pain is part of the process, but those who push through find something far greater: resilience, mastery, and a level of greatness that only endurance can uncover.

Grit embodies the relentless spirit of perseverance—an unwavering commitment that transforms ordinary efforts into extraordinary outcomes. It is more than mere determination; it is endurance fortified by passion and resilience. When obstacles arise, and comfort fades away, grit is what compels us to stay the course and push forward.

True excellence demands that we navigate discomfort, setbacks, and moments of doubt. Pain and struggle are not mere obstacles but necessary milestones on the path to mastery.

**Those with grit understand that temporary pain
is often a precursor to lasting achievement.**

They recognize that growth is rarely comfortable; greatness rarely emerges from ease.

Developing grit requires embracing challenges as opportunities for growth rather than barriers to success. It involves fostering patience, maintaining focus through distractions, and choosing commitment over convenience. With each difficulty faced, the capacity for perseverance deepens, building character, resilience, and a powerful inner strength. Ultimately, grit reveals a deeper truth: those who persist through the toughest storms are rewarded not only with achievement but with profound personal transformation and lasting greatness.

OPPORTUNITY

A chance to do more is a chance to do less of nothing.

Opportunity isn't just about gain—it's about avoiding stagnation. Every moment holds potential. Doing nothing guarantees no progress, while taking even a small step forward opens new possibilities. When opportunity knocks, answer—it may not come again.

Opportunity is the intersection of awareness and action—moments that hold potential if seized deliberately. While some see opportunity as a fortunate event or lucky circumstance, it is more accurately viewed as a proactive stance toward life's possibilities. Each moment that presents itself, no matter how small, contains seeds that could grow into something remarkable, provided we nurture them with intention and action.

Inaction leads to stagnation, a silent thief that robs us of progress and fulfillment. To remain idle when opportunity arises is to willingly let potential slip away, choosing comfort or fear over the growth and reward that await just beyond hesitation. By contrast, even a single step forward—no matter how modest—can create momentum, revealing possibilities previously unseen.

Recognizing opportunity requires attentiveness and an open mind.

Opportunities rarely announce themselves loudly; more often, they whisper subtly, blending into the ordinary until someone brave enough decides to act. Taking decisive action in these quiet moments differentiates those who merely exist from those who truly thrive. Embracing opportunity means not only responding when the chance arises but actively creating the circumstances for new opportunities to appear. The choice is clear: seize the moment and turn potential into reality or remain passive and allow possibility to fade quietly into nothingness.

EQUANIMITY

When action leads to chaos, inaction may be the path to preserving sanity.

Not every battle is worth fighting. Sometimes, restraint is the best strategy. When the world spirals into disorder, stepping back can be an act of wisdom. Equanimity is about balance—knowing when to engage and when to let go to maintain inner peace.

Equanimity is the quiet strength found in measured response. It is the careful balance between action and stillness, a skillful approach to navigating life's turbulence without losing emotional stability. True equanimity does not mean indifference; rather, it is the mastery of choosing when to engage and when to consciously hold back, maintaining clarity amid turmoil.

In moments when impulse and reaction threaten to escalate disorder, stepping back becomes the most courageous and rational choice. It's an acknowledgment that not every challenge demands immediate resolution or aggressive confrontation.

Equanimity thrives when emotions run high—it's the ability to calmly assess, thoughtfully respond, or sometimes wisely refrain from any reaction at all.

Practicing equanimity involves training oneself to observe rather than react impulsively. It is rooted in emotional intelligence, patience, and acceptance that some situations must unfold without interference. By developing inner calmness, we retain control over our mental space, allowing rational thought and measured responses to guide our actions. Ultimately, equanimity is the art of preserving sanity and inner peace, particularly in moments when the chaos outside threatens to overwhelm.

TENSION

When swords are drawn and tempers flare, prepare for chaos—it's in the air.

C onflict, once ignited, is hard to contain. When tension reaches a breaking point, chaos is inevitable. Awareness of this can help us navigate difficult situations with caution, patience, or readiness for what's to come. The best defense is preparation.

Tension is often a precursor to conflict—a clear indication that patience has worn thin, and peace hangs by a thread. Its that tangible energy felt in charged atmospheres, a silent warning signaling imminent confrontation. Recognizing tension when it begins to build is essential to managing or mitigating the chaos that often follows. Once conflict erupts, the aftermath rarely remains predictable or easily controlled.

Awareness is critical. Sensing escalating tension provides a crucial advantage—time to prepare, strategize, or possibly diffuse what's approaching. Preparation can mean different things: mental readiness, emotional calmness, or even practical actions to safeguard oneself or others.

The ability to perceive tension early is itself a skill, cultivated through attentive observation and emotional intelligence.

Navigating tension requires discernment and flexibility. Sometimes diplomacy and dialogue are enough to relieve pressure; other times, cautious vigilance or strategic retreat is the prudent course. In some scenarios, confrontation becomes unavoidable. In these cases, acknowledging tension allows one to enter conflict clear-headed, grounded, and strategically prepared. Ultimately, the ability to recognize and navigate tension is a powerful asset, turning potential chaos into controlled and meaningful action.

EROSION

When time is our currency, we become wealthy growing poorer with each passing day.

T ime is both abundant and fleeting. While we may feel rich in moments, each passing second is spent and cannot be reclaimed. True wealth is not in money, but in how we use our time. Spend it wisely, before it runs out.

Erosion symbolizes the subtle, relentless force of time in our lives. At first glance, time seems endless—an abundant resource available for us to spend lavishly. Yet, with each passing moment, our supply diminishes irreversibly, gradually eroding the reservoir we once considered infinite. Unlike financial wealth, time offers no replenishments, no deposits, no reversals; every second spent is permanently withdrawn.

Understanding erosion means appreciating that our most valuable currency isn't something we hold in our hands but the intangible moments slipping quietly through our fingers. Every interaction, pursuit, or choice either adds value or wastes this precious resource.

> **Recognizing the erosion of time invites reflection on priorities: Are we investing in experiences and relationships that matter, or are we squandering our wealth on trivial pursuits?**

Managing this erosion involves intentional living—consciously choosing how we allocate each moment. It is about trading fleeting pleasures for lasting fulfillment, avoiding regret by investing in meaningful experiences, authentic connections, and personal growth. In this mindful stewardship, we transform the inevitable erosion of time into a legacy of significance, creating a wealth of memories and impact that transcend its passage.

MOTIVATION

The fear of failure is the incubator for inaction.

F ear is the greatest thief of progress. The hesitation to act often comes from a deep-rooted fear of failing. But failure itself isn't the enemy—inaction is. Those who never try will never succeed. Transform fear into fuel, and let motivation drive you forward.

Motivation is the internal fire that transforms fear into action. At its heart lies an undeniable truth: hesitation and inaction stem from a paralyzing fear of failure. Yet failure, in reality, is not the destructive force we imagine; it is the silence of inaction—the refusal to even attempt—that truly limits growth. By succumbing to fear, we relinquish potential, dreams, and future achievements to the shadows of doubt.

Confronting this fear requires understanding its source. Fear often stems from past disappointments, societal expectations, or self-imposed pressures. Acknowledging these factors equips us to challenge them constructively. Real motivation arises when we harness fear as a catalyst rather than a barrier, viewing each risk as a steppingstone toward our goals. It means redefining failure not as defeat, but as evidence of courage, resilience, and the willingness to engage fully in life's challenges.

> **True motivation doesn't eliminate fear—it channels it. It compels us forward, even when outcomes are uncertain.**

Each attempt made despite fear strengthens our capacity to act, builds confidence, and diminishes hesitation over time. Eventually, motivation becomes second nature, guiding us not away from failure, but boldly through it, toward meaningful progress and fulfillment.

WISDOM

Make time for friends and even foes and leverage the opportunity to learn from both.

L essons come from unexpected places. Wisdom isn't found only in allies—it can also come from adversaries. Every interaction offers a chance to learn, grow, and refine our perspective. Those who listen, even to their opposition, gain an edge that ignorance can never provide.

Wisdom is not confined to familiar spaces or friendly interactions; it flourishes where perspectives diverge. True wisdom involves a willingness to step beyond comfort zones, engaging openly not just with friends who echo our beliefs, but also with foes who challenge and provoke our thoughts. Every individual, regardless of their relationship to us, offers unique experiences, insights, and understandings shaped by their own distinct journeys.

By actively seeking dialogue with those who disagree or even oppose us, we cultivate deeper empathy and understanding. Such exchanges reveal blind spots in our own reasoning, helping us refine our beliefs and decisions.

Wisdom teaches us humility—recognizing that we don't hold all the answers. It invites curiosity, patience, and openness to the complex mosaic of human thought.

Ultimately, wisdom lies in our ability to see beyond labels of friend or foe. Instead of avoiding conflict, it urges us to embrace conversations that test our assumptions. Each person we encounter becomes a teacher, and each conversation, a lesson in growth. In this open-hearted approach, we become wiser, more adaptive, and better equipped to navigate life's complexities.

DETERMINISM

If tomorrow was yesterday and yesterday was today, then the future is written, and history has already spoken.

Time moves in cycles but understanding the past shapes how we navigate the future. History's influence is inevitable. While we cannot rewrite what has been, we can learn from it. The future is only predetermined if we refuse to change our course.

Determinism suggests a world where outcomes seem fixed, governed by patterns and echoes of the past. It reminds us that historical events aren't isolated incidents—they ripple through time, shaping present choices and future possibilities. This cycle isn't about fate alone but emphasizes the profound influence of past actions and choices on current and future outcomes.

Understanding determinism involves recognizing patterns of behavior—our personal histories, societal cycles, and recurring mistakes—and making conscious decisions to alter our course. Rather than resigning ourselves to repeating past errors, we have the power to interrupt these cycles by learning and evolving.

Awareness of determinism allows us to confront the habits and beliefs that trap us in repeated loops of outcome, enabling intentional redirection toward new possibilities.

While history might hint at what's likely, it doesn't dictate what must be. Embracing this concept empowers us to become active participants rather than passive observers. By thoughtfully examining the past, we equip ourselves to shape a future not bound by inevitability but guided by deliberate and conscious choice.

ADAPTABILITY

There is no such thing as a final solution. They are all efforts towards a better outcome.

Progress is an ongoing process, not a fixed destination. Flexibility in problem-solving is essential. There will never be a perfect, permanent solution—only better versions of what came before. Those who adapt will continue moving forward, while those who seek finality will be left behind.

Adaptability is rooted in the understanding that life is continuously evolving, and challenges are never permanently resolved. Instead, solutions serve as steppingstones, paving the way toward continuous improvement. This mindset recognizes that circumstances shift, priorities change, and even the best-laid plans require reevaluation and revision. Rigid adherence to a single approach inevitably leads to stagnation or even failure when unexpected changes emerge.

True adaptability means embracing uncertainty as an opportunity for innovation rather than an obstacle to overcome.

It's the willingness to reevaluate, to listen openly, and adjust courses without attachment to past methods or beliefs. In business, relationships, or personal goals, being adaptable is often what distinguishes sustained success from fleeting achievement. Those who see every challenge as a chance to grow and learn build resilience and remain relevant in a world that never stands still.

In essence, adaptability is about humility and agility. Accepting that no solution is ever final enables constant growth and encourages a lifelong commitment to improvement. Each adjustment, no matter how small, is progress—moving forward incrementally, continuously, toward something better.

THE POWER WITHIN

L ife's greatest journeys are often the ones we begin without full knowledge of the path ahead. They are marked not by predictable progress but by resilience, adaptability, and the persistent pursuit of our goals despite uncertainties. Throughout the voyage toward success, challenges will undoubtedly emerge, presenting moments that test our courage, commitment, and inner strength. It is precisely in these moments of uncertainty and challenge that our true potential is forged, shaped by our willingness to act boldly, think strategically, and persist relentlessly.

The path toward achieving your goals requires you to adopt a proactive mindset. Success does not reward hesitation—it favors those willing to seize opportunities without waiting for perfect timing. Every day presents a fresh opportunity to step forward, to act decisively, and to make meaningful progress. The courage to move even when conditions aren't ideal defines the essence of genuine progress and sustained momentum.

Yet, as we advance boldly, it's essential to balance optimism with caution. Wisdom lies not just in relentless action but in thoughtful preparation and clear-sighted strategies. Approaching life with careful consideration and calculated risk ensures that enthusiasm is complemented by practicality. Through a balanced approach, you fortify yourself against setbacks, building resilience through a foundation of mindful preparedness.

Trust becomes crucial when strategies reach their limits, when your voice alone cannot pave the way. At these critical junctures, belief in yourself, in the process, and in the higher forces at play provides strength. This faith is not passive—it represents active confidence, reinforcing your ability to withstand doubt and uncertainty. Trust is the bridge between your actions and your outcomes, calming internal chaos and bringing clarity to your purpose.

Throughout this journey, recognizing and harnessing the true value of your time and resources becomes paramount. Each moment invested wisely in growth, learning, and self-reflection compounds over time, laying a solid foundation for long-term achievements. Prioritize your energies on actions that align closely with your values, ensuring every step taken is purposeful and meaningful.

Resilience is your ally, empowering you to stand firm in the face of adversity. It's not merely about recovering from setbacks; true resilience anticipates difficulties, turning potential setbacks into stepping stones for future success. Coupled with the choice to surround yourself with diverse perspectives, you enhance your capacity to adapt, innovate, and evolve. Diversity of thought brings creativity to problem-solving and insight into life's complexities, enabling you to navigate the unexpected with grace.

Persistence combined with discipline propels you forward, even through the toughest challenges. The continuous effort, dedication, and unwavering grit you bring to your goals make every success more rewarding and every challenge more manageable. Persistence is not just repeated action—it's driven by mindful intention, reinforcing your commitment to achieving extraordinary outcomes.

Your personal growth depends significantly on embracing change and stepping beyond your comfort zone. Exploring new paths, taking calculated risks, and adapting swiftly to life's shifts help reveal the depth and breadth of your capabilities. With each new challenge comes an opportunity to refine your skills, deepen your understanding, and expand your horizons. Boldness is about taking decisive action even without guarantees, knowing that the true rewards often lie beyond immediate sight.

As you progress, mindfulness and awareness ground you in the present, fostering clarity and ensuring each step aligns with your overarching vision. Reflecting regularly helps you recognize the growth you've achieved, reinforcing your journey's significance and strengthening your resolve. The power of mindfulness lies in its ability to transform even ordinary experiences into extraordinary insights, ensuring every moment is leveraged for maximum growth.

Moreover, maintaining integrity and honesty throughout your journey safeguards your sense of self and builds credibility with those around you. It establishes trust, enhances your reputation, and fosters meaningful connections. True freedom emerges not from external validation but from staying authentic, transparent, and consistent with your principles and values.

Balance is equally vital. It allows you to stay grounded even as you reach ambitiously for your dreams. A balanced approach ensures you are neither overwhelmed by life's challenges nor blinded by its opportunities. It empowers you to sustain your energy, preserve your well-being, and maintain an enduring commitment to your goals.

Investing in self-care fortifies your mental, physical, and emotional health, creating a sustainable path toward long-term success. Caring for yourself ensures you remain energized, clear-minded, and focused, fully capable of tackling every hurdle and embracing every joy that comes your way. Self-care is not indulgent—it's strategic, ensuring your ability to thrive rather than merely survive.

The ultimate message of your journey is one of boundless optimism and possibility. Embrace the lessons of tranquility and peace; let quiet moments recharge your spirit and refuel your drive. Let inspiration guide you, and allow your vision to expand beyond present limitations. With vigilance, ingenuity, and an unwavering commitment to growth, you become unstoppable.

Your journey embodies the essence of hope and optimism, proving that despite life's complexities, every dream is achievable with determination, dedication, and resilience. Every step forward—no matter how small—matters deeply, shaping your trajectory toward ultimate fulfillment. Your path may wind, your courage may waver, but your commitment to growth, enriched by experience and fortified by a relentless spirit, will ensure that every challenge met transforms into a story of triumph.

Above all, know this—you are capable of achieving extraordinary things. Your goals are within your reach, waiting only for your decision to claim them. This journey, rich with lessons, strength, and self-discovery, serves as your greatest guide and most trusted companion. Believe deeply, act boldly, persist relentlessly, and know without doubt—you can do anything.

ABOUT THE AUTHOR

E zekiel Daniel is an author, life coach, and visionary leader passionate about guiding individuals toward personal excellence and transformative growth. With an extensive educational background, Ezekiel holds a Master of Science in Emergency Management from Capella University (2020), a Master of Science in Post-Secondary Education specializing in Instructional Technology from Troy University (2007), and a Master of Science in Healthcare Management, also from Troy University (2005). Additionally, he earned a Bachelor of Science in Occupational Education from Wayland Baptist University (2004), demonstrating a strong commitment to lifelong learning and professional development.

He is the published author of "CO2: The Evolution of A New World," an insightful exploration into societal transformation and environmental consciousness, showcasing his deep commitment to strategic thought and innovative problem-solving. In "Changing Bad," Ezekiel continues this dedication, providing readers with empowering insights and practical guidance to cultivate resilience, embrace purposeful action, and confidently navigate life's uncertainties.

Outside of writing, Ezekiel finds joy in creative problem-solving within interior design, creating custom solutions that maximize space and enhance the functionality and beauty of living environments. His passion for design and drive to inspire others underscores his holistic approach to life, work, and creativity.

CLOSING THOUGHTS

As you conclude your journey through these pages, remember: true empowerment comes not from what you read but from what you apply — consistently.

Embrace change. Take calculated risks. Lead with integrity. Persist through adversity.

Continue cultivating your mind, nourishing your soul, and pursuing your purpose — boldly and unapologetically. Your potential is boundless. Your capacity for growth is limited only by the depth of your imagination and the strength of your resolve.

You are ready.

Let nothing hold you back.

ACKNOWLEDGMENTS

I extend heartfelt gratitude to everyone who has walked with me on this journey. To my family and friends for their endless support and to mentors whose wisdom and guidance have profoundly influenced my path. Your belief in me and commitment to my growth have made Changing Bad: Harnessing the Power of Motivation a reality.

Special thanks to the dedicated readers whose hunger for knowledge and self-improvement inspires me daily.

Thank you all sincerely.